More (Advanced) Lessons in Comprehension

More (Advanced) Lessons in Comprehension

Expanding Students' Understanding of All Types of Texts

FRANK SERAFINI
SUZETTE YOUNGS

HEINEMANN • PORTSMOUTH, NH

Heinemann
361 Hanover Street
Portsmouth, NH 03801–3912
www.heinemann.com

Offices and agents throughout the world

Cataloging-in-Publication data is on file at the Library of Congress.
ISBN-13: 978-0-325-01121-9
ISBN-10: 0-325-01121-4

Editor: Wendy Murray
Production: Vicki Kasabian
Cover design: Jenny Jensen Greenleaf
Cover image © Corbis Photography
Typesetter: House of Equations, Inc.
Manufacturing: Steve Bernier

Printed in the United States of America on acid-free paper
12 11 10 09 08   ML   1 2 3 4 5

This book is dedicated to my good friend Dr. Rich Coles. Our intellectual conversations for the past twenty years have made me a better educator, and the good times we have had traveling across North America have made me a better human being. Thanks for sharing with me your knowledge and experiences as a literacy educator. The students that passed through your classroom are better people because of your dedication to their education and well-being. You prove that intelligence and a sense of humor work well together.

Frank Serafini

I would like to dedicate this book to my brother, Frank. I know it seems weird since we wrote this book together, but to me it really does make sense. About two years ago, we sat in a pub in Chicago. While drinking a few margaritas, I convinced you to let me write this book with you. You even made me submit an official proposal on a cocktail napkin! Thank you for having faith in me as a writer and allowing me to share in the creation of this wonderful resource for teachers. You inspire me and guide me everyday. You are a generous scholar. I am proud to be your sister, and I look forward to the many adventures that lie ahead.

Suzette Youngs

Contents

Introduction

In the foreword to *Lessons in Comprehension* (2004), P. David Pearson said to think of my series of lessons as a menu, a scope without a sequence, a set of possibilities for developing one's own effective instructional practices. I appreciated David's insights as I set forth in *More (Advanced) Lessons in Comprehension* to expand the menu of lessons and widen the scope of instructional possibilities. My goal in this book is to provide upper elementary and middle school teachers and literacy educators with a kaleidoscope of effective lessons that will expand their instructional repertoires, taking them deeper into the comprehension process to explore and support more sophisticated ways of reading and thinking.

Not only will *More (Advanced) Lessons in Comprehension* provide me an opportunity to share some lessons that I was unable to fit into the first book, it allows me to share with you my latest thinking on reading comprehension instruction. For the past several years, I have been spending time in intermediate and middle school classrooms observing gifted literacy educators teach comprehension lessons and support students' interpretive abilities. I have been conducting workshops across Canada and the United States on issues concerning reading comprehension and instruction, and have been teaching graduate and undergraduate courses in literacy education and children's literature. All of these experiences have helped shape the content and format of the lessons provided in *More (Advanced) Lessons in Comprehension*.

This time on my journey into the reading workshop, I have once again enlisted the help of my fellow educator, and sibling, Suzette Youngs. You may remember reading about her classroom and teaching from her wonderful "Windows on the Workshop" contained in our book *Around the Reading Workshop in 180 Days* (2006). Throughout the book, Suzette's vignettes provided classroom teachers with a window into her reading lessons and instructional practices. Suzette's detailed explanations of how she incorporated my suggestions into her teaching made her reading workshop come to life for our readers.

Suzette has occasionally joked around that she "brought the heart" to our book, and I have to agree it may be true. Her wonderful vignettes allowed teachers to see how my ideas played out in an actual classroom. By doing so, she also endowed teachers with "poetic license," some ownership and flexibility in how they implemented the instructional practices and reading workshop framework that I conceptualized. By describing her own classroom practices, and demonstrating how to take my ideas and adapt them to fit her own students' needs,

Suzette made it OK for teachers to use my ideas as simply suggestions and as a framework or an instructional guide. Suzette showed teachers how to take my ideas and adapt them to fit their classrooms.

For *More (Advanced) Lessons in Comprehension*, I have asked Suzette to draw upon her extensive experience as an intermediate grade teacher, plumb her files, and select some of the most effective and innovative lessons from her teaching that I know you will find extremely valuable. She brings a different lens to the creation of this book, and I hope you will find the additions helpful.

The primary difference between the lessons contained in *More (Advanced) Lessons in Comprehension* and my previous book *Lessons in Comprehension* is the level of sophistication of the lessons contained in this volume. I felt that we needed to provide upper elementary and middle school teachers with more complex, in-depth lessons for expanding their instructional repertoire. Drawing on literary, semiotic, and critical theories, *More (Advanced) Lessons in Comprehension* presents the reader with lessons that delve deeper into reading comprehension processes and challenges teachers and students alike to expand their interpretive abilities.

I see the lessons contained in this book as exhibitions of effective teaching. In the foreword to *Lessons in Comprehension*, David Pearson said that I wanted teachers to "adapt, not adopt" these lessons. Truer words could not have been written. It is my hope that you will use *More (Advanced) Lessons in Comprehension* to expand your instructional repertoire and provide the necessary support for developing proficient and sophisticated young readers.

Frank Serafini

More (Advanced) Lessons in Comprehension

CHAPTER 1

Rethinking Reading Comprehension and Instruction

> Literacy is the flexible and sustainable mastery
> of a repertoire of practices.
> —ALLAN LUKE AND PETER FREEBODY,
> "Shaping the Social Practices of Reading"

Comprehending, Not Comprehension

Before we delve in to our instructional ideas, we should probably spend some time explaining what we mean by reading comprehension. We made a couple of these points in the opening sections of *Around the Reading Workshop in 180 Days*. First, we want teachers to focus their attention on *comprehending*, not *comprehension*. *Comprehending* is an action verb and connotes a process, whereas *comprehension* is a noun, suggesting a thing or commodity. Too often our instruction, assessments, and classroom discussions seem to favor the notion of comprehension as commodity, focusing on carrying away or measuring some amount of knowledge or attribute from a reading event. Let's focus instead on helping our students with the *process* of making sense, not simply the residuals of reading.

To offer a definition, we see comprehending as *a process of actively constructing meaning in transaction with texts in a particular social context*. We believe that reading is both an individual cognitive process and a social process that derives meaning from the contexts in which it occurs. Comprehending, then, is a sustained cognitive and social activity that involves the successful orchestration of language and thinking processes. These processes begin with the noticing or perception of textual and visual elements and ends with the construction and reconsideration of meanings. We use the plural *meanings* to suggest that the meanings constructed by readers are temporary, multiple, and open to revision. This definition, which was constructed through our own research and experiences, the writings of various reading and literary theorists and reading researchers, including Louise Rosenblatt, Frank Smith, David Pearson, Kathleen McCormick, Allan Luke, and Robert Scholes, informs all the lessons in this book.

Here are several additional assumptions on which our definition of reading comprehension is based:

❖ There is no unmediated access to texts. Texts are read by readers that come to the process with particular experiences, understandings, and knowledge. The book does not read itself, it must be read by someone.

❖ Meanings and interpretations are always socially constructed and historically embedded in local and particular contexts. In other words, we never read in a vacuum. Readers always read some particular text, at some particular time and place, with an author and the language and history of the reader's culture and experiences involved in the process.

❖ The construction of interpretations is never a disinterested process. Meanings and interpretations are always derived in political, social, historical, and cultural contexts. In other words, particular interpretations or meanings work toward particular interests. Each and every time we read a text we bring our own experiences and our histories of who we are to the reading event. These sociocultural factors affect how we read, what we read, and the meanings and interpretations we construct with texts.

❖ There is no transcendent authority (objective presence) to refer to when attempting to establish the "truth" of a particular reading. We choose to acknowledge particular readings as more or less viable. Main ideas are constructed, not discovered by close examination of the text. In other words, when someone in authority, for example a test maker, decides what the main idea of a text selection, this idea is endorsed by that authority. The author consciously and unconsciously puts forth main ideas, but even the author is not the sole arbiter of truth. Each reader brings his own truth to the authors' text as he interprets it. Thus, main ideas are co-created, not found.

❖ Every classroom is a site for the production of meanings. Every interpretive community has some allegiance to a particular literary tradition or perspective, and each literary practice functions to close off possible readings (meanings) from other perspectives. In some classrooms, being able to find the one, correct main idea may be endorsed, whereas in another classroom, being able to defend alternative interpretations may be valued. Each classroom has its own set of rules for determining what is valued as a reader and expresses these values through the expectations set and the experiences provided and endorsed.

We believe there is no singular, objective truth contained within a text, but many truths, each with its own authority and its own warrants for viability. Additionally, since there is no objective meaning of a text, comprehension is concerned with the *viability* of interpretations, how interpretations become useful, and the social negotiations of these various meanings. There are multiple meanings and interpretations that arise in transactions with texts, some viable, some not. The reading workshop, with its constituent readers, becomes the social milieu in which the viability of a particular interpretation is discussed, challenged, and warranted. Reading comprehension instruction ought to focus on understanding texts from a variety of perspectives and learning how these perspectives endorse and dismiss particular meanings and interpretations.

In order for readers to construct meaning in transaction with texts, they must understand the codes and conventions of written language, become familiar with the vocabulary used by the author, and be able to connect the text with their own experiences and background knowledge. Jonathan Culler (1997) suggests one's *literary competence* or comprehension is based on a reader's understandings of the codes and conventions used by the author. Schema theorists believe that reading comprehension is the ability of a reader to accommodate and assimilate new information from a text into one's existing schemas and background knowledge.

In every reading event there are four major perspectives that come into play:

❖ the text

❖ the reader

❖ the author

❖ the context (both immediate and sociocultural)

Each of the prevailing literary theories highlights one of these perspectives, while still maintaining the presence of the others. For example, reader-response theories, as the name suggests, focus on the role of the reader in constructing meaning, their experiences, cultures, and psychological makeup. Historical criticism focuses on the life and times of the author to understand how the text was created and the possible meanings available. Socioculturally based literary theorists focus, not on the reader as an individual agent acting independently, but on the culture and contexts in which the reader resides and operates. The New Critics focus on the text in and of itself. This perspective has dominated literature education for many decades. Each and every literary perspective focuses on one aspect of the reading event, trying to understand how that component plays into the meanings constructed and available, while downplaying the other components.

For us, the literal text is the *point of departure* in comprehending and interpreting a text, not the finish line. Reading is about appropriating or contextualizing the meanings constructed in transaction with texts into one's own experiences or knowledge base. It is this connection between the text we encounter and the world in which we live that is the focus of many of our lessons described throughout the book. The text is where we begin, not where we end.

Taking Reading Comprehension Instruction Beyond the Literal

One of the biggest challenges we see in reading comprehension instruction is helping teachers, and novice readers, get past decoding, oral performance, and literal recall in their discussions and instructional experiences. It's not that we want readers to stop paying attention to the actual written text, nor do we want them to be unable to read a text fluently and with intonation. But we have to be aware that when we constantly focus our instructional lens on decoding a text accurately, rather than focusing on thinking and interpretation, we may be inadvertently sending the wrong message. In elevating the literal text over interpretation in class discussions and assessments, we privilege the text over the reader, and this, too, sends the unfortunate message to students that their ideas don't count, they aren't part of the deal.

We end up creating readers that can say words aloud accurately, but have no idea what the text means. These readers pay dearly as they mature, for as students advance through school and encounter more complex texts, decoding becomes less and less an effective predictor or indicator of one's comprehension abilities. Our instructional focus should go "beyond the literal" to help readers to comprehend texts and construct viable interpretations to share and negotiate with other members of one's community of readers. This is our intention for each and every lesson throughout this book.

In the first *Lessons in Comprehension*, Frank listed five essential characteristics of reading comprehension instruction, namely: (1) Deliberate, (2) Responsive, (3) Explicit, (4) Relevant, and (5) Research-Based. We believe these are still extremely important and relevant to our discussion here. Therefore, we are including a summary of those characteristics for you in this book as well.

Effective Comprehension Lessons Are:
1. **Deliberate**—Our lessons should be deliberate, meaning we have articulated ahead of time a purpose or goal we are trying to achieve. Our goal may be quite general—for example, to instill a love of reading—or quite specific—to demonstrate a specific comprehension strategy. The important thing is that each lesson is rationally planned; we have legitimate reasons for conducting it and we can articulate what these reasons are.

2. **Responsive**—We need to base our lessons on our students' needs and abilities, meaning we draw on our observations of them as readers, our knowledge of the reading process, and our sense of which class experiences will work best to move students forward. In other words, the lessons are designed to respond to what students need next. Sometimes referred to as "teaching in the zone of proximal development" (Vygotsky 1978) responsive teaching holds the teacher's knowledge base in high regard. It's the teacher's insight about students that matters, the teacher's familiarity with the reading research, community expectations, and the district and state curriculum mandates—not a commercial scope and sequence.

3. **Explicit**—The language we use with students and our demonstrations have to be clear and explicit, always pitched to clarify what we are teaching. To accomplish this, we have to ask students if they understand what we are talking about and watch them when they are applying what they have learned. This recursive process of teaching and assessing will help make our comprehension lessons more effective. Although explicit instruction does not guarantee learning, the more we check for understanding and help students understand what we mean, the greater the chance that students will be able to apply what they are learning.

4. **Relevant**—The comprehension lessons we provide need to relate to the types of reading that readers do in the real world, not just in school. Students consider a lesson relevant (and engaging) when they understand its purpose and can see how it relates to their world and their goals.

5. **Research-Based**—Research should inform our teaching practices and provide information about what is effective. However, our instructional practices should be based on a *wide range* of research perspectives and methodologies. We need to be careful that the research base we use to direct our instructional practices is not reduced to such a point that important instructional decisions are based on a single vision of reading, teaching, and learning.

To build upon the characteristics put forth in *Lessons in Comprehension*, we would like to offer a few more considerations that we have been thinking about since that book was published. To begin, ways of comprehending texts should be discussed and demonstrated to students in a variety of settings, utilizing a variety of texts and instructional experiences. In addition to one-on-one conferences and instruction, there are three primary contexts in which reading instruction occurs: (1) whole-group discussion and instruction, (2) comprehension strategy groups, and (3) literature study groups. In comprehension strategy groups, the focus is on reading and the reading strategies being demonstrated. In literature study groups, the primary focus is on the piece of literature being shared. However, we believe that the experiences of reading and discussing literature in study groups does in fact develop readers' abilities even if that is not the primary focus of the discussion.

We have used the word *demonstration* to describe the types of interactions that we expect teachers to enact during comprehension lessons. We don't want the word to be misleading. A demonstration can often connote a minimal amount of participation by those observing the demonstration. This would be unfortunate. The comprehension demonstrations should be considered *exhibitions*, shared experiences that invite students to get involved with the ideas being demonstrated. These exhibitions demand active listening and a willingness to explore the ideas demonstrated on one's own. We want our students to get involved in the exhibitions as quickly as possible. We don't want the focus of our demonstrations to remain on what *we* do, but what we want *students* to do.

There are two additional considerations that we would like to discuss before moving on to the actual lessons in comprehension. The first is the notion that as we conduct lessons in comprehension (or any lessons for that matter), we think about the lesson's instructional trajectory—the future effects—of each lesson. What occurs after a lesson is completed, the *residuals* of our teaching if you will, are just as important as the lesson itself. We ask ourselves, "How did the lesson I just present affect readers' subsequent interactions with texts? How will the lesson I just conducted improve readers' abilities to make sense of texts they have not yet encountered?"

The second consideration is a rethinking of the Gradual Release of Responsibility (GRR) model popularized by Pearson and Gallagher (1983). In this model, the amount of responsibility the teacher has in a reading event is released to the student as the student accepts control of the reading. We now turn to a more in-depth discussion of these two considerations.

Instructional Trajectory

Too often, we focus on the procedures and resources rather than the effects or consequences of our reading comprehension lessons. In other words, we need to consider what happens after the lesson is over, or the *trajectory* of the lessons we exhibit. *Instructional trajectory* is a concept that looks at the effects of a lesson to consider the range, authenticity, and depth these lessons provide.

Our conception of instructional trajectory has several components. First, the *range* of a comprehension lesson considers the variety of contexts an individual lesson will support readers in the future. Effective lessons in comprehension should work across a variety of contexts, enabling novice readers to comprehend a variety of texts, for a variety of purposes. We don't mean to imply that these lessons actually become "universal strategies" that readers simply apply every time they encounter a text. What we mean is that our lessons should "teach forward." The focus of our lessons should be how the strategies we demonstrate help readers understand the texts they have not yet encountered, not simply those texts being read at a particular moment.

Second, lessons should be examined for their *authenticity* or *relevance*. By this we mean that lessons should prepare novice readers to use strategies that will help them in reading events they will encounter in the world, not just in school. Some comprehension lessons seem to prepare readers solely for school-based literacy events, not those that occur in the world outside school. Learning how to build a diorama or construct a mobile based on a book character may help students garner approval in some classrooms, but we strongly doubt it will help them effectively perform in any literate events once outside the school grounds. Our lessons have to be relevant to the literacies of our students' lives both in and out of school.

Third, lessons should also be examined for their ability to help students generate interpretations before, during, and after reading, or what I would call the lessons' *interpretive focus*. In other words, we need to consider the *depth* of a particular lesson. The goal of comprehension lessons should be helping readers comprehend texts. This may sound redundant, but we have seen too many lessons that stop short of the goal of comprehending. We need to keep our "eye on the prize," so to speak. In this case, the prize is helping students make sense of what they are reading.

For example, in one classroom Frank observed, a teacher presented several lessons that focused on *how* to predict, not *why* to predict. It got to the point that all the students were doing was stopping throughout each book being read and predicting what might come next. The teacher would then read on to see who was correct. Predicting was reduced to seeing who was right, not who was making sense or being strategic. Although we would agree that prediction may help in comprehending some texts, in some particular contexts, the goal of our lessons should not be to simply get good at predicting. The goal is to get good at *using* predicting to make sense of texts. Our lessons need to keep the focus on generating interpretations, not the isolated use of a particular strategy.

Another example is the creation of classroom charts or artifacts during comprehension lessons. In many of our lessons, we include the charts we have used to support the focus of a particular lesson. These charts serve as an "audit trail" of where the lessons have been and allow teachers to build upon these instructional foundations in subsequent lessons. However, we need to remember that the goal of a comprehension lesson is not to get better at creating charts. The goal is to *use* charts to extend thinking and discussion, and deepen learning. These charts need to be conceptualized as a "thinking device" used to help readers comprehend and reflect on what has been read.

We need to consider whether our lessons help change and improve the way teachers and students think, talk about, comprehend, and respond to what they are reading. The primary goal of the reading workshop instructional framework that we have been developing over the past decade or more is to help novice readers and teachers talk about texts in more meaningful ways and comprehend what they read from a variety of theoretical perspectives.

At this point, you might be asking, "Where does one can find evidence that any of this instructional trajectory is occurring?" We believe that we find evidence of the residual effects of our lessons in the writing our students do in their reader-response logs; the level of sophistication of the discussions we have in whole-class settings and literature study groups; the strategies our readers employ when reading independently; and the growth we observe during our comprehension strategy groups. It is not enough to say that one has taught a certain strategy. It is more important to consider whether that strategy is effective in developing the types of readers we want to support, and whether there is evidence that our lessons are being taken up by the readers in our classes.

Reconsidering the Gradual Release of Responsibility Model

Since Pearson and Gallagher (1983) wrote about the Gradual Release of Responsibility (GRR) model, it has served as a framework for many literacy instructional programs and approaches to developing comprehension lessons. The GRR model is based on the transfer of responsibility for a particular learning task (e.g., reading a text) from the teacher or more proficient reader to the novice reader or student. The focus of this model is the level of responsibility the teacher must maintain to ensure a successful learning outcome or completion of a particular task. In other words, it is primarily concerned with the amount of responsibility the teacher *releases* to the student. It assumes that responsibility initially resides with the teacher and is given over during instruction to the students or learners. By only focusing on the amount of responsibility released by a teacher, this becomes a model that focuses on teaching rather than learning. We want to recalibrate the model, to ensure that the *learning* that is taking place is brought into the equation. We think it's often overlooked because we so intensely focus on the teacher's level of responsibility. The student's level of responsibility, or independence, is cast almost as an outcome rather than as something to cultivate and monitor throughout the application of this teaching/learning model.

In the opening chapter of *Lessons in Comprehension*, Frank wrote about an Emerging Expertise (EE) model. The EE model focused on the student's emerging expertise or involvement in the learning experience, rather than focusing solely on the release of responsibility from the teacher. The focus in this model is on the student and the amount of responsibility the student *accepts*. In other words, the focus is on learning, not simply on teaching. We believe that both the teacher's and student's involvement are equally important components in any learning situation and this consideration must remain a vital part of any instructional model. We also believe that both learning and teaching were part of Pearson and Gallagher's original model, but the teaching side of the model has become the primary focus at times, and we want to be sure that learning, or the emerging expertise of the novice reader, is not left out of the model.

The amount of involvement of the student, and the level of support offered by the teacher, or the amount of responsibility released, has also been referred to as *scaffolding* by Wood, Bruner, and Ross (1976), and many others. In their seminal article, they discuss three primary considerations of scaffolding: (1) allowing a learner to do what they are capable of individually, (2) offering support for what a learner can almost do on their own, and (3) doing for learners what they cannot do on their own. Drawing on these three considerations, it remains the teacher's primary responsibility for maintaining the quality of the learning experiences provided students; however, the amount of support being offered is determined by what a child can do with help from the teacher, not what they can do independently. Vygotsky's Zone of Proximal Development (ZPD) always presupposed a novice and teacher working together, where the ZPD of the child is determined in this milieu, not when the student is working independently. In some assessment instruments, it is assumed that tests given to students can determine their ZPD. This is a misunderstanding of Vygotsky's theories.

In order to maintain the effectiveness of a particular learning experience, teachers need to shift the amount of support in response to the needs of a particular learner in the context of the learning event. It is not a predetermined level of support that can be simply calculated by a single assessment, nor does the level of support necessarily remain stable throughout the lesson or learning experience. The level of support a teacher provides must be in response to the amount of "expertise" a learner develops. The optimal amount of support or scaffold can only be determined in the context of the actual learning event through close observation of the learner's ability and competence. We do not know what learners are capable of doing with our support until we get them involved in an actual learning task.

The scaffolds we provide can be considered *within tasks*, for example, how much response we give a reader in a particular shared reading experience, or *across tasks*, for example, when teachers decide to read a text aloud to students, rather than asking them to read it independently. What we want to provide students, both within tasks and across tasks, is a *manageable amount of challenge*. We don't want students to become overly frustrated; however, we want them presented with enough challenge to require student involvement and thinking.

This level of challenge will differ for each reader and cannot be accurately assessed outside the actual learning experience. It must be assessed in the context of the learning experience and is based on the child's developing competence or expertise. Because of this, teachers' close observation of student literacy behaviors is paramount. What an individual can do with the help of a more capable other can only be understood in the actual context of learning something new. When reading with a child, we can begin to understand what they can do when we call their attention to things they miss themselves, for example, particular elements in a text or illustration. We cannot determine what they can do with our help if we are not in fact in the process of providing that help.

Some Closing Thoughts

The goal of reading instruction, and indeed the goal of the lessons contained in the book, is to create self-sufficient, self-regulated, independent readers capable of bring a variety of perspectives to the texts they encounter in order to make sense of what they read. Because of this, all reading instructional practices should be conducted *in service of meaning*. In other words, whether teachers are developing readers' decoding skills or vocabularies, teaching readers to visualize or predict, or helping someone choose an appropriate text for independent reading, the objective of these lessons should be constructing meaning in transaction with the texts students are reading. Teachers cannot sit idly by and hope that readers are making sense of what they read. The research is overwhelmingly in favor of direct explanation and instruction in comprehension strategies. It is the role of the classroom teacher to demonstrate what proficient readers do when they read, provide opportunities for readers to acquire appropriate reading comprehension strategies, and listen and observe readers to determine how they are using these strategies to make sense of what they read.

We would like to close this section by making two assertions. First, the *quality* of the classroom teacher, not the instructional program, is the primary variable in determining the effectiveness of a comprehensive reading program. This assertion is often hidden beneath the glitz and packaging of many commercial programs. It is not the quality of the resource, but the skill and experience of the teacher that makes reading and writing come alive in today's classrooms.

Second, no *significant* changes in instructional practices will occur until corresponding changes take place in one's theoretical understandings. In other words, unless we rethink why we do what we do in the name of literacy education and instruction, most changes will be cosmetic, superficial. The resources teachers select may change, or the daily schedule may be rearranged to accommodate new programs, but the core of one's instructional practices will remain intact without developing one's theoretical understandings.

What do these assertions mean for school reform efforts focusing on literacy education? We believe it means that we need to invest time, resources, and effort into professional development models that balance pedagogical innovations with theoretical understandings. Change occurs when teachers understand more about effective instructional practices, based on sound theoretical foundations and current research, that support literacy development.

There are three key principles of professional development that form the basis of our work with teachers and literacy specialists: access and opportunity, choice and ownership, and dialogue and reflection. First, teachers need access to quality literature and reading materials, opportunities to share ideas with other teachers, and time and support to enact new instructional practices. Second, teachers need to have choice and voice in their professional experiences in order to take ownership and responsibility for their development. Finally, teachers need time to reflect upon and discuss their instructional decisions and practices with other educators.

In addition, we need to help classroom teachers, administrators, and literacy specialists develop a *preferred vision* for the instructional practices and learning environments they create in their schools and classrooms. It is our role to help teachers articulate what they want their instructional practices and learning environments to look like, sound like, and focus on. In order to develop a preferred vision, teachers must be able to critically examine their teaching practices based on current theoretical understandings. Growth without direction is confusion, and direction without growth is learned helplessness.

CHAPTER 2

How This Book Is Organized

Like *Lessons in Comprehension* (Serafini 2004), we have organized our comprehension lessons into eight strands. Each of the strands are held together by a common theme or focus for the reading workshop. The comprehension lessons contained in this book address the International Reading Association (IRA) and National Council Teachers of English (NCTE) standards for reading and the language arts. Each individual lesson is a description and series of instructional recommendations for teachers to adapt to their particular settings and students. Each of the eight strands will contain eight individual lessons that focus on various aspects of reading comprehension. We will begin each strand with a brief introduction, a description of the types of lessons included, and how this particular series of lessons fit into the overall framework of the reading workshop.

The eight strands are:

1. Getting Beyond Traditional Responses to Literature
This strand will focus on meaningful ways for students to respond to literature, expanding traditional notions of written response. Readers will be shown a variety of modes to express their interpretations of what they read. Lessons will highlight performance, image, voice, artistic expression, movement, and multiple connections to literature as possible forms of response.

2. Expanding Interpretive Repertoires
This strand will focus on instructional strategies and practices that help teachers lead more effective discussions. These strategies can be used in small-group or whole-class discussions. The goal of these strategies is to help students develop their interpretive repertoires by challenging them to reconsider a text from new and varied perspectives.

3. Reconsidering Teacher Talk and Classroom Interactions
This strand will provide lessons and suggestions to rethink the traditional Initiate–Respond–Evaluate (IRE) interaction pattern found in many classrooms today. The focus of these lessons is the language of instruction, the talk that is part and parcel of every lesson teachers provide. Techniques like providing uptake, demonstrating active listening, and platforming will be included.

4. Reading Across Genres
This strand will provide explicit instruction in ways to approach, understand, and explore a variety of genres. These lessons will focus on attending to audience, purpose, perspective,

the affordances and constraints of genre, and approaching and reading multiple genre picturebooks.

5. Comprehending Novels and Extended Texts

This strand will focus on strategies for working with longer texts, in particular novels, in the reading workshop. Many of the lessons included in other sections utilize picturebooks, poetry, and shorter texts in each lesson. This strand will provide teachers with some strategies for keeping track of ideas across longer texts, how to code texts for discussion, and how to relate novels to picturebooks and poetry to expand discussion possibilities.

6. Critical Reading in the Social Sciences

This strand will focus on instructional strategies that will help students read websites, textbooks, historical fiction, and other multimodal documents. With the plethora of expository texts and historical documents available, it is necessary for students to become critical readers so they may determine the validity and viability of particular pieces found not only on the Internet but also in primary source documents and classroom textbooks. These lessons will include a variety of teacher and student think-alouds that will demonstrate a range of reading strategies necessary to comprehend these complex reading materials.

7. Comprehending Visual Images

This strand will focus on reading the images included in magazines, expository texts, picturebooks, and other multimedia. Drawing on the work of Kress and van Leeuwen (1996), the lessons in this strand will help teachers to understand the components of visual design, the use of framing and composition, and the role of color and focus in constructing meaning with visual images.

8. Interpreting Texts Through Literary Theories

This strand will focus on eight different literary theories and provide suggestions for how these theories can be used to expand readers' interpretive abilities. These lessons will draw upon feminist, psychoanalytical, critical, and historical theories to expand the perspectives that readers bring to the texts they encounter.

Each lesson in comprehension will include the following components:

1. Title: a brief label for the comprehension lesson
2. The Challenge: observations about why we think this particular reading comprehension lesson may address particular students' needs
3. Our Intentions: the rationale for conducting this lesson
4. Lesson Overview: a description of the comprehension lesson or series of lessons and how they operate
5. Language of Instruction: a narrative explaining how the lesson might have unfolded and examples of the language used during instruction
6. Instructional Trajectory: suggestions on how to extend these lessons across time in the reading workshop
7. Classroom Artifacts: examples of the types of charts and artifacts created during the lesson, where applicable

8. Closing Comments: an opportunity for us to include any concerns or ideas that may be important for teachers to consider

In addition to these components, we will include, where applicable, lists of children's literature and other resources used to support each lesson. It is our intention that each lesson can stand on its own and can be used in any order that teachers feel works for them. However, in The Challenge section of each lesson, we share why we think the lesson was necessary at a particular time in our reading workshops. Also, in the Instructional Trajectory section we explain how the lesson could be used as a foundation for subsequent learning experience. But again, these lessons are not designed to be done in the order listed, nor are they to be blindly followed. These are not scripts to follow, rather recipes we encourage you to adapt. We want teachers to be reflective, to consider why certain lessons are needed, and to be thoughtful decision makers who provide the supports necessary to help young readers make sense of the texts and images they encounter.

In addition to the resources provided in each lesson, Frank has created a website, **www.frankserafini.com**, to support teachers and literacy specialists engaged in workshop approaches to literacy instruction. You'll find numerous resources: book lists, professional readings, classroom strategies, position statements concerning various issues in literacy education, and numerous links to other literacy websites and resources. We encourage you to go to the website for additional resources and information, especially the list of thematic booklists.

Getting Beyond Traditional Responses to Literature

Responding to literature is a ubiquitous practice in elementary classrooms. Students are often limited by the ways they are expected to respond to their reading, because they are never required to extend their response beyond writing book reports or filling in worksheets. The lessons in this strand challenge classroom teachers to move beyond these traditional response activities and provide opportunities for students to construct more sophisticated interpretations and deeper meanings as they interact with, and respond to, literature.

With literal recall activities, readers are asked to simply recite the text back to the teacher in order to demonstrate they have comprehended what they have read. This is a limited vision of comprehension. The text itself is privileged over the thinking and meanings constructed by the students. As our definition or vision of comprehension expands, so must the ways that we invite our readers to exhibit their understandings.

We can't overemphasize here that the response activity is never *an end in itself*, but rather an opportunity to explore literature in a variety of ways. The two primary goals of these literature response experiences is first to help readers understand how and why they respond to literature the way they do, and second to extend the responses readers construct and support them as they consider a variety of perspectives on what they are reading.

Students are asked to think in new and more complex ways when they are asked to transfer their understandings of the literature they read and represent these understandings through another sign system. Several of the lessons in this strand ask readers to "transmediate" their understandings from one mode of representation to another. For example, a student might work from a written text to a Powerpoint presentation, a skit, or a three-dimensional model or visual image. Requiring readers to extend their thinking beyond one mode of representation provides opportunities for readers to demonstrate their understandings in new and more sophisticated ways.

The comprehension lessons in this section include:

1.1 Drawing as a Response to Literature

1.2 Literary Dinner Party

1.3 Multimodal Responses to Literature

Drawing as a Response to Literature

The Challenge: Many young readers naturally respond to literature by drawing the setting, characters, and other story elements. Building on this proclivity, teachers frequently ask readers to draw their favorite part of a story. In this lesson, we ramp up this classic lesson by helping children to use drawing to express their analytical thinking about a text. In the same way we give readers the tools to analyze written text, we also want to give readers access to the tools of visual images. These visual tools not only extend students' interpretation, they help students represent these interpretations as well.

Our Intentions: Drawing in response to literature is a common strategy, but we don't want it to remain at a literal level. For example, having students simply draw their favorite character may not add to their interpretations of the text. Drawing as a response strategy should support students in moving past literal meaning to delve into their interpretations of a text. In this lesson, children will use drawing and sketches to represent their interpretations and consciously use the design elements of visual images to communicate their ideas about a particular chapter book.

Lesson Overview: Using the book *Locomotion* by Jacqueline Woodson (2003), this lesson focuses on attending to visual design elements to enhance drawing as a response to literature. After reading and discussing *Locomotion*, the teacher will demonstrate through a *draw-aloud* how to utilize elements of visual design to enhance a drawing that represents the teacher's interpretation of the text (see Figure 1.1). A draw-aloud is an instructional strategy where the teacher draws their ideas on a chart in front of the class and thinks aloud about how and why she is utilizing various visual design elements to represent her interpretations.

Language of Instruction: Good morning, Readers! We finished reading *Locomotion* a few days ago and have had some very interesting discussions. Today, I would like for us to utilize the visual design elements that we have been studying (see Lessons 7.2 and 7.3) to enhance our responses to literature. I would like for us to incorporate these design elements into the drawings we will create as we respond to the chapter book *Locomotion*. In the past I know that I have asked you to draw your favorite part of a piece of literature, but today I would like you to utilize your knowledge of visual design elements to make your drawings even more powerful. To begin, let's review some of the design elements we have attended to so far, for example, color, shape, line, composition, size of images, framing, white space, and perspective. We have used these tools to *analyze* various images in the picturebooks we have read and now we are going to use them to *represent* our interpretations of *Locomotion*.

We have all of these elements available for us to use, so we will need to make decisions about what we put into our picture to impact how our viewers understand our drawings. On a piece of chart paper, I am going to sketch some possibilities for my response to *Locomotion*. We need to realize that each drawing will be different as each interpretation is different, and with a chapter book there are endless response possibilities.

The idea of framing is an interesting element to consider for responding to this novel. The poetry used throughout the text and the first-person narrative suggests that we are privileged to all of the main characters' thoughts and that a full-page bleed might represent this notion. However, there are times in the book when I feel that Lonnie is trapped in his thoughts, and so I might use a lot of white space around my picture to represent this idea. I am going to draw a picture of Lonnie and his sister Lilly, because she is all that he has left for family besides Miss Edna, and he is willing to do anything to see her and be with her. Lonnie's relationship with Lilly defines who he is. Lilly's new Mother judges him and decides when and where he gets to see her so in many ways I think she defines who he is as well. So, I am going to use some white space around this picture to demonstrate how Lonnie is constrained by society and his situation (see Figure 1.1).

I am going to use a line in the middle of my drawing to represent Lilly's mother as she separates the two and I am going to make the line bold to show the differences in their status. I am also going to give the mother some red because I think she has power in this scene. Lilly is going to wear all white to appear angelic. I am going to place Lonnie at the

FIG. 1.1
Draw-Aloud Example

bottom of the page as he is grounded in the everyday. What else could we use from our knowledge of visual elements to enhance this drawing? [*Students share ideas and come up and add to the drawing.*]

Now, let's create our own drawing as a response to this piece of literature. You may use any and all of the visual design elements we have studied that make sense for your picture. When you feel that you are done, I would like you to swap pictures with a partner and have them *read* your drawing using what we know about visual design. We will then come back as a whole group and share all of the pictures and how they represent our understandings of the book.

Instructional Trajectory: Readers are surrounded by visual images on a daily basis. The more they know about the design elements used to create illustrations in picturebooks, the better equipped they will be able to read these images and make sense of them. This lesson creates opportunities for students to utilize images to represent their thinking at a much deeper and more meaningful level. Students may choose to respond through drawing in their literature response notebooks, using a variety of visual design elements to represent their thinking.

Classroom Artifacts: After the teacher completes a think-aloud and draw-aloud demonstrating her interpretations of the book *Locomotion*, students will create a drawing that represents their understandings. These will be displayed and used as a vehicle for extending discussion.

Closing Comments: This lesson helps children use drawing as a viable way to express their thoughts. It will expand students' responses to literature and may affect students' drawing and art projects as well. This lesson also creates opportunities for those who struggle with words to represent their ideas through art.

Literary Dinner Party

The Challenge: Students are commonly asked to make intertextual connections during literature discussions, but too often the connections teachers ask them to make are superficial, relating to characters' names or physical characteristics. In this activity, we push the envelope a bit, asking students to *interpret* characters, to go beyond superficial attributes and make sense of the dynamic nature of fictional characters and their relationships to one another.

Our Intentions: In this lesson, we will use intertextual connections to help students understand various characters portrayed in picturebooks in a unit of study on building community. Students will choose a character to portray and will consider ways this character might interact with other characters at an imaginary dinner party. Students will be asked to take on the persona of one character by rereading the text and researching how that person would think and converse based on the information in the book. Students will also need to understand something about the other characters at the dinner party to know how they might think and behave.

Lesson Overview: Using various picturebooks from a Building Community unit of study constructed and utilized in the beginning of the year (see an example in Serafini and Youngs 2006), students will choose one character to portray, conduct research into this character's traits, and be prepared to respond as this character might. The teacher will launch this lesson by modeling one character for the whole class, then students will choose from the numerous characters available from the unit and follow the same format.

Language of Instruction: Good morning, Readers! As a culminating activity to our building community unit, we are going to think about the character Tacky from *Tacky the Penguin* by Helen Lester (1988) and create an imaginary dialogue with the other characters invited to a dinner party. On a chart behind me, I have provided a list of characters from the books we have read in this unit that we might invite to an imaginary dinner party. Let me start by asking this question, "Based on the characters listed in this unit, what should we have for dinner? What kinds of food should be served? What kinds of drinks should we have?"

Let me give you an example by discussing the character of Tacky and demonstrate how you might prepare for an imaginary dinner party. Let's start by thinking about Tacky as a character. What other characters in attendance would Tacky like to hang out with, and what might he say to them? How might he greet the other characters at the party? For example, I think he might hang out with the Straight Line (from *The Straight Line Wonder*

[Fox 1997]), because they are both strong characters that don't give in to peer pressure. I think they might like being together since they don't worry about their friends who only liked them when they saved the day or became famous. I also think that Tacky would like to be introduced to Smudge (from *Voices in the Park* [Browne 2001]). They have similar qualities and they seem to really enjoy life. I also think he would probably stay away from the Mother in *Voices in the Park* because she is a control freak, and wants to dominate everyone around her. She might cast a shadow over Tacky's outlook on life.

Now, I would like you to think about a character you would like to be. After you have decided on your character, we will ask ourselves some questions to help us think about your character (see Figure 1.2). In small groups create a seating chart for the characters you have selected, then we will come back as a whole group and negotiate a final seating chart for next week's dinner party (see Figure 1.3).

Instructional Trajectory:	This dinner party activity could be adapted to help students interpret historical figures and other real-world characters like scientists and inventors. Any group of characters, fictional or nonfictional, could be invited to dinner. Over time, we would expect to see deeper discussions of character—a character's salient traits, their motivations or agendas—in both the whole-group discussions and individual students' literature response notebooks.
Classroom Artifacts:	Students will create a list of character traits, and some examples of what their character might say, how they might act, and what they might think. In addition, they can talk about how their character would be dressed and what they might enjoy eating.
Closing Comments:	The interpretive potential for the dinner party is limitless. Students need to interpret their own character as well as project how other characters might interact with them. Students and teacher will be able to take time to reflect on the dinner party at the end and to engage in an in-depth discussion as to how the character traits can and will affect their own lives as they consider the real world and the implications of building a community of learners.

FIG. 1.2
Questions to Ask in Preparing to Be a Character

- ❖ What characters might want to sit next to each other and why?
- ❖ How would your character dress for the party?
- ❖ What might your character say to Tacky if they were seated together?
- ❖ What would your character want to eat?
- ❖ How would your character act at the party?
- ❖ Is your character happy, sad, angry, etc.?

FIG. 1.3
*Possible Characters
Attending the Dinner
Party*

Chrysanthemum (from Henkes' *Chrysanthemum*)

Tacky the Penguin (from Lester's *Tacky the Penguin*)

Lilly (from Henkes' *Lilly's Purple Plastic Purse*)

The Straight Line (from Fox's *The Straight Line Wonder*)

Mr. and Mrs. Piggott (from Browne's *Piggybook*)

Simon and Patrick (from Browne's *Piggybook*)

Owen (from Henkes' *Owen*)

Smudge (from Browne's *Voices in the Park*)

The Mother (from Browne's *Voices in the Park*)

Multimodal Responses to Literature

The Challenge: This lesson can be very helpful for readers as they explore a variety of literature response modes, including photography, graphics, illustrations, websites, Powerpoint, and so on. Often, teachers direct children to a single mode of response, for example, a character web, rather than allowing the relationship between reader and literature to suggest the type of response that would be the most effective in representing the student's interpretations.

Our Intentions: This lesson is designed to help readers understand that various response modes have both *affordances* and *constraints*—that is, strengths and limitations—and that choosing a particular mode is a response in itself. Our goal is for students to analyze a variety of modes so that they can then be more purposeful in selecting one that best fits their needs and understandings. Choosing different response modes will require students to interact with the text in different ways.

Lesson Overview: Using the picturebook *Sister Anne's Hands* by Marybeth Lorbiecki (1998), we will introduce and analyze a variety of possible response modes and discuss the affordances and constraints of each mode. In small groups, students will decide on a particular response mode to complete and present to the class. Students should attend to their understandings of the picturebook as well as to how the response mode represents their interpretations.

Language of Instruction: Good morning, Readers! Today I am going to read the book *Sister Anne's Hands*. When we are done reading this wonderful, yet challenging picturebook we are going to discuss a variety of ways to respond. [*Read and discuss book.*] Now that we have read the book, let's discuss some possibilities and some familiar ways to respond to literature. One way that we can respond to *Sister Anne's Hands* is through drawing. When we respond through drawing, we allow our interpretations to become visual representations. We use colors, lines, shapes, and shape placement to represent our interpretations. We may choose to experiment with motifs or depict symbolism we think the author and illustrator have embedded in the book. Or we might create a collage of images, drawing on the many aspects of history that were presented in this picturebook.

Another way to express our interpretation is through tableaux. In tableaux, readers decide on a scene in the book, or some part of your interpretation, and a small group of students strike a pose. It is very much like looking at a painting. There is no movement or talking. The idea is that you decide on some aspect of the book that you would like to "paint," and then you position your body to represent your interpretations. Then the audience will discuss what the scene is about, and then each student will get a chance to share their interpretations and how the scene portrayed meanings.

Another possibility is giving voices to the characters that don't speak, or who have little power in the book. For example, in *Sister Anne's Hands*, there are many characters that play an important part in the book but do not say anything; we come to know them only through their actions or reactions to Sister Anne. For this response mode, you give words to those characters that were only described, like the angry parents or the school board. In this response mode, you have a chance to give secondary characters a voice.

A fourth possibility is a written response. In this response mode, you will complete a Noticings, Connections, Wonderings chart (see Lesson 2.1). Your group can discuss the book and then record your noticings and ideas from the text and illustrations, record any personal or intertextual connections you have made, and share any wonderings you might still have about the book.

A final possibility is creating a "sound effects group." If *Sister Anne's Hands* were turned into a movie what sound effects might you include? Think about background voices, music, and the noises from the actions of characters or any words or sounds that would come from the events in the story. The purpose of this response mode is to think about the impact that sound has on our interpretations. For example, as we watch a scary movie and the music starts, we just know something scary is going to happen. Sound portrays meaning beyond the words and actions of the characters. In this response mode your group will discuss possible interpretations and then create sounds to accompany the reading of the text.

Before you decide the response mode that you would like to try I would like you to discuss the book and what it means in your small groups. As your group discusses and negotiates your interpretations, choose a mode that will match what you are thinking about the book. Over the next two days we will have each group share their response modes. As each group is sharing we will talk about the affordances and constraints of each type of response. In other words, there are things that one way of responding can express about *Sister Anne's Hands* that others cannot. While you are creating these responses, I invite each group to keep a journal of the strengths and challenges of your response mode. We will discuss our interpretations and evaluations of the book again and how each response mode highlighted different aspects of our interpretations.

| Instructional Trajectory: | This lesson will affect the way students respond to literature for the rest of the year. Not only are students interpreting literature but also they are critically analyzing the kind of response that is most able to reveal their full thinking and connection to a text. Students will be more apt to read and respond more deeply if they have a bunch of response modes to dip into, and if they come to find that they have an enduring preference for, say, a visual response, this can only help them as readers. For literature |

study groups that include a presentation, this lesson and follow-up lessons will be very helpful for students deciding which mode will best represent their interpretations. Students might even decide to use a combination of response modes, as no one mode may express all of their understandings.

Classroom Artifacts: Each mode will be presented and small groups will keep a journal of the strengths and limitations of each response mode. Students might also create classroom charts to describe and compare the different response modes and display these in the classroom for future reference.

Closing Comments: Asking children to analyze modes of response can be challenging. Typically, a teacher assigns the creative response activity with little or no attention to how the mode can enhance or inhibit the reader's interpretation. A response mode should be able to deepen readers' responses in meaningful ways, as meaning is always the focus of any reader response. We hope this lesson gives teachers the opportunity to avoid too much reliance on written response assignments as windows onto their students' interpretive thinking.

Constructing Literary Board Games

The Challenge: Playing board games or creating ones on particular texts has been a teacher and student favorite for generations. Here, we offer a lesson that helps us avoid a common pitfall, where the game becomes little more than a box of literal recall questions. As with any good response to literature, the trick is to incorporate a way for the players to respond on *various levels*, not just by remembering "fun facts" about a book.

Our Intentions: Our goal for this lesson is to make constructing a board game a viable response to literature. Board games will be something the rest of the class can play if they have read the book. In order to construct a quality board game, children will need to begin by engaging deeply with a piece of literature. Children enjoy playing games, so let's use this fact to help them connect to the texts they read and construct more sophisticated interpretations.

Lesson Overview: Using a book the entire class has read, we will design a board game for the class to play containing literal and inferential questions. We will use *The Tale of Despereaux* by Kate DiCamillo (2003) as a demonstration, and will discuss the various aspects of constructing a board game.

Language of Instruction: Good morning, Readers! Having already read *The Tale of Despereaux* together, I thought we would talk a little bit about how to make a board game as a response mode to literature. You all love playing board games in our classroom and making a game in response to literature can be an engaging activity. Game designers need to consider many elements of a book in order to create a game. First, I want us to consider how we might mix trivia questions, or answers we can point to directly in the book, with questions that involve interpreting, making connections, as well as responding personally. You may use some literal questions, but we also want the questions in the game to go beyond a Trivial Pursuit–type challenge.

Let me begin by demonstrating what I would think about when creating a board game for *The Tale of Despereaux*. First, the plot. How might this structure help me to design the game? There are four stories in the book so the playing board might have four worlds that a player has to travel through—Despereaux's, Miggery Sow's, Roscuro's, and the fourth world could be the Soup World where all the stories come together at the end of the book and soup is once again eaten in the kingdom. I might also consider: How can I represent the characters' traits and their unique stories? What are the symbolic aspects of the book? How might these be included? How can the narrator's voice be represented?

In addition, I might include light and dark areas on the board to mark the themes of good and evil. The trail that the players follow could be characterized by a red line to represent Despereaux's quest. All the questions could begin with the word *Reader* like DiCamillo did in the book making the reader feel a part of the story. What other aspects of the story do you think might be important to include? [*Class discussion ensues.*]

In any game there has to be some sort of challenge. In a literature-based board game, it seems to make sense to ask questions. The danger lies in that if we only ask literal questions, there might be a tendency to have only right or wrong answers and we want to avoid that. So, it will be important for players to have a book on hand so that they may defend their answers with ideas from the text and from personal interpretations of the text that go beyond literal meanings.

We might want to ask questions in categories. For example, we could ask questions that require players to make connections to their own lives, to other books, and to the world. Players might use literary elements to analyze particular parts of the book, or just give an interpretation to the overall meaning or particular parts. In a game like this the other players might act as judges as to the viability of the player's response. Moving to the next square will depend on whether the response makes sense, rather than looking for a correct answer.

For *The Tale of Despereaux* , it might be effective to utilize drama, drawing, connections, and personal response cards. In this way the game matches the theme of the book and players can give a response rather than an answer. Let's draw a possible game board and think about some possible questions.

Instructional Trajectory: Any book students read and enjoy is appropriate for this lesson. Just remember that creating a board game is an a complex endeavor and might take a long time to complete. Also, use your judgment. There will be some books that just don't seem to lend themselves to this activity.

Classroom Artifacts: The board game itself will be an artifact that can be played, discussed, redesigned, and used as a point of discussion.

Closing Comments: Playing games is a wonderful way to build community and to learn at the same time. When students construct a board game they are not only delving into the literature but also problem solving, strategizing, discussing, and presenting information all at the same time. Students really need to understand a piece of literature to make it into a quality board game. Discussing and negotiating themes, character growth and change, determining plot structure all require an intimate relationship with any piece of literature. So it almost goes without saying that most of the richest learning takes place as the game is developed.

Expanding Readers' Theatre

The Challenge:
Readers' Theatre is a widely used response strategy designed to enhance fluency and enjoyment of a particular text. Many times students are given scripts or students create the script from excerpts of the text they are reading. During Readers' Theatre not only do we want students to think about the literal script, we want them to consider their understandings of characters' motives, themes of the story, symbols, issues of power, and characters' identities.

Our Intentions:
In this lesson, we want students to consider Readers' Theatre as another mode of response to literature. By selecting specific words and lines from the text and adding their interpretations to the literal text, students are able to represent their understandings of the text in a much richer way. In Readers' Theatre, students will incorporate movement, voice, words, and body position as ways of representing meanings.

Lesson Overview:
Using the book *Voices in the Park* by Anthony Browne (2001), we will negotiate part of a Readers' Theatre script as a whole class, and then small groups will write and perform their own scripts. Having previously read and discussed the text, students will able to focus on their interpretations to support their creation of the scripts and their actions during Readers' Theatre.

Language of Instruction:
Good morning, Readers! We have been reading and discussing *Voices in the Park* by Anthony Browne and have analyzed the text and illustrations for the past few days. Today, I am going to share a new way to look at Readers' Theatre with you. In the past we have used Readers' Theatre to enjoy the sounds of poetry, as well as for fluency practice. Today, we are going to utilize movement, voice, and body position to construct deeper interpretations of this picturebook. I would like for us to think about the text and the visual images that might be important to include in a Readers' Theatre script.

First, let's consider the actual text for the script as we think about all the literary and visual design elements we have discussed and our analysis of this book over the past few days. Think about each voice and how we might create a script that captures the emotions and changes in character. I would also like for us to think about the illustrations, what meanings they convey, and how we might represent these meanings through Readers' Theatre.

Second, I would like us to think about body positions for acting out this script. Where might we position the readers? Which characters have power? How might we position each reader to show power and status? Do any of the readers need to move during the reading to show changes in their character?

Let's discuss one of the characters together as an example of how you might discuss the book in your small groups. What words might be important to utilize in considering the mother's character? What words can you take from the text and what words might you include from your own mind to represent your interpretations of her character? How might we position this character during the Readers' Theatre? Let's begin a chart to help us think about the characters (see Figure 1.4). We will begin the chart together to get you going and then in small groups you will work on a script for your own group to present to the class

Instructional Trajectory: Readers' Theatre is a widely used instructional approach. Our twist on it is that we emphasize how crucial it is for students to have sufficient time to read and discuss the text before performing the book for the class. Extending the possibilities for Readers' Theatre allows students to use it to interpret any text, whether it is a chapter book or picturebook. In addition, students may use this approach to present books read in their literature discussion groups. During this lesson students may begin to think about how characters are related to one another and may also apply this to historic concepts and characters as well. Readers' Theatre is also a great approach for showing how various historical figures had power over others, or how an historical event might be depicted.

Classroom Artifacts: Classroom charts can be created to serve as an example (see Figure 1.4) and then small groups may add their ideas to the whole-class chart. Individual groups can create a script for their interpretations and the actual performance can be videotaped or audiotaped for further reflection and interpretation.

FIG. 1.4
Analyzing Characters for Readers' Theatre

May be copied for classroom use. © 2008 by Frank Serafini and Suzette Youngs, from *More (Advanced) Lessons in Comprehension*. Portsmouth, NH: Heinemann.

Character	Words from the text or images important to character	Our own words to show interpretation	Placement of character and possible nonverbal cues?	Props
Mother	It was time to take our pedigree Labrador and our son for a walk Neat in her dress, nose in the air	This man sitting next to me on the bench is frightful and beneath me	Sit above the other characters, no eye contact with any character, do not touch any characters	Red hat
Charles				

Closing Comments: Readers' Theatre is a multifaceted avenue for students to explore important issues in literature and to think deeply about how characters are portrayed. Allowing students to add their own words to the original text, and to think about how characters' identities might be portrayed gives students the power to negotiate their understandings of a text.

Multigenre Responses to Literature

The Challenge: Different genres provide different insights and rewards for readers. Fairy tales, for example, can't help but stir up thoughts about good and evil, kindness and greed, love versus treachery, wealth and poverty. Contemporary fiction may yield for students more immediate personal connections to their daily lives, from a book's pop culture details to its themes. Reading history books may get us thinking in more "big picture" ways. Each genre has unique structures, elements, and formats that convey the narrative, factual information, and so on. Deeply understanding the characteristics of a variety of genres can enhance readers' experience and facility with any genre. In addition, multiple genres can be used to support readers' responses to the literature they encounter. For example, we might have students imagine which genres characters might draw upon to tell their own stories. In other words, responding across a variety of genres requires students to step into the characters' lives and represent their understandings through the structures of a particular genre.

Our Intentions: Our goal is to have students consider a character in a real-world setting and to think about what they might say, do, or write to other characters in the book or even people who exist in our present world. Students will create a piece of writing that draws upon the elements and structures of a particular genre to represent their understandings of a character from a piece of literature.

Lesson Overview: In this lesson we are going to read the picturebook *Piggybook* by Anthony Browne (1986) and brainstorm a list of genres that characters might write or genres someone might write about them. Students will choose a character, create a writing piece, and then present it to the class. When these pieces are all completed we will compile their responses in a book for our classroom library.

Language of Instruction: Good morning, Readers! Yesterday we read *Piggybook* by Anthony Browne. Today, I am going to read it again and discuss some new ideas. I want you to think about what genres the characters might write or what someone else might write about the characters or events that happen in the story. Let me give you an example. The mother in this story may have written in a journal about her family problems, or she might have written a more extensive note to her husband explaining why she was leaving. [*Read and discuss.*]

Now that we have read the story, let's think about the characters, the events in the story, the social issues we have discussed, any connections to our world or other texts, and any personal connections you have made to the characters. Let's consider what writing

FIG. 1.5
*Possible Genres for
Responding to* Piggybook

Mrs. Piggott: Letter to her family, help wanted ads, journal, diary, self-help books, appearance on the Dr. Phil show, how-to manual about relationships, car repair magazines, Dear Abby letter, advice from a counselor.

Mr. Piggott: Business papers, newspaper, business reports, lists for his wife, business travel arrangements, papers in his briefcase, daily planner, tax reports, bills, cookbooks.

Simon and Patrick: Thank-you note to mom, homework assignments, books on adventure, drawings, model airplane directions, Christmas and birthday wish lists, to-do lists for mom, cookbooks

might take place in response to this book and generate a list of possible genres different characters might use to represent their stories (see Figure 1.5).

Each of you may choose one of the genres we have listed for responding to the text or create your own. Pick one that you feel will help you to express your interpretations of the text and will expand your thinking about *Piggybook*. When we are finished, we will share these responses. Please be prepared to share how your writing project helped you to understand the character you chose or any aspects of the book you thought were important.

**Instructional
Trajectory:** This writing project helps readers to think deeply about characters as they imagine what genres these characters might use to extend their stories. The actual selection of the genre tells a lot about students' interpretations of a character, any themes, or events in the story. This type of written response can also be used to respond to biographies and historical documents.

Classroom Artifacts: Genre writing projects and a list of genres the characters might utilize would be the primary artifacts for this lesson. These can be collected for the classroom library.

Closing Comments: Transmediating the elements or characters from one story to another is a complex cognitive process. Students need to have an extensive understanding of the elements and structures of a variety of genres if this experience is to be successful. Extending the plot of a story or character's traits and motives into another genre and setting requires readers to deepen their understandings and construct more sophisticated interpretations of the literature they experience.

Dear Charlotte

The Challenge: Letter writing in response to literature has been a favored response activity in many elementary and middle school classrooms. Typically, students write to a favorite character or to the author asking essential questions about the story, sharing their ideas about the text. In and of itself, writing letters does not ensure that students are being asked to reflect and think deeply about a particular story. It is important for students to use any response activity as a tool to further their thinking, generate new interpretations, and negotiate meanings with other readers.

Our Intentions: Utilizing letter writing, students will explore the conflicts found within a particular book and analyze how these conflicts affect the main characters and events in the story.

Lesson Overview: Readers will use what they know about Charlotte and other characters in *Charlotte's Web* (White 1952) to construct a "Dear Charlotte" advice column. Each student will choose one character and write a letter to Charlotte seeking advice on some issue they experience in the story. Each student will then respond to another student's letter from the perspective of Charlotte.

Language of Instruction: Good morning, Readers! We just finished reading and discussing the book *Charlotte's Web*. In our discussions over the past week I noticed how we kept thinking about Charlotte as an important character in the story. We noticed how she sometimes acted like a mother and friend, and how she was connected to each character in some way. You also noticed how she acted as a sort of counselor to Wilbur. Based on our discussions, I thought it would be interesting if we wrote advice columns for the characters and events in the story.

An advice column is where someone writes to a person at a newspaper, magazine, or website asking advice on a variety of issues. Some advice columns give advice about relationships, family problems, gardening, cooking, parenting, and a whole bunch of other topics. The person who answers these letters in the column is considered an expert on giving advice to his or her readers. People read these columns to see how the columnist answers their or other readers' letters. Before we consider writing our own letters, let's read some different advice columns and chart out our ideas on what we might write about and how we might write them. [*Students and teacher share a variety of advice columns.*]

Now that we have some ideas about advice columns, let's think about different characters in *Charlotte's Web* and what advice they might need from Charlotte. There are many

FIG. 1.6
*Dear Charlotte Letter
Topics*

Wilbur

❖ How to live in a barn

❖ How to move on when a friend dies

❖ How to boost one's self-esteem

❖ How to get along without Fern

❖ How to spin a web

❖ How to avoid being the Christmas ham

❖ How to take care of spiders

Fern

❖ How to get my father to keep from killing Wilbur

❖ How to get my parents to agree to keep a pig in the house

❖ How to keep people from thinking someone is crazy for talking to animals

❖ How to get a boy to like someone

Templeton

❖ How to get out of saving Wilbur

❖ How to find the best scraps of food

❖ How to manipulate everyone around you to do what you want without doing anything for him or her

❖ How to have animals accept me for the nasty rat that I am

conflicts within this story that we might identify and discuss. As we identify a particular problem, we can write a letter to Charlotte asking her for advice on how to solve it. For example, we have discussed and identified one of Wilbur's conflicts as his need to become a much stronger character. We might write a letter to Charlotte asking her advice on how to become more self-reliant. Let's brainstorm some other possible conflicts or ideas for a letter (see Figure 1.6).

OK, let's choose one of these ideas and think about how Charlotte might respond. [*Teacher models letter to Charlotte and Charlotte's letter in return.*] When you are writing your letters you might want to consider how a character changed in the story. You might also want to consider how you will support the ideas in your letters from the information in the text or from personal experiences. In other words, the letters need to make sense for the characters that are writing them to or for. As we share our letters, you might be asked to discuss how you came up with your letter topic and how you can support your interpretations. OK, let's each pick a character and give it a try!

Instructional Trajectory: Analyzing conflicts and character development are important strategies for readers to employ as they read and interpret literature. This activity is creative and requires readers to analyze the connections between characters and how various conflicts affect the plot of a story. We hope to see students attending to various conflicts in their future reading-response logs as well as classroom discussions.

Classroom Artifacts: Once students finish their letters they could be compiled in a class book for students to read and enjoy. A sample of actual advice columns should be provided as models and for discussion.

Closing Comments: Analyzing and interpreting various literary elements in literature is at the heart of the reading workshop. This letter-writing activity gives students experience analyzing conflict and characterization, as well as themes and story resolutions. Minor characters' actions and their conflicts affect the main character and the story in subtle ways, and analysis of these can help students comprehend the story on deeper levels.

Investigating Response Through Powerpoint

The Challenge: Written text cannot always capture what children want to say about a piece of literature. Students live and learn in a world filled with images. Outside the classroom, they use colors, images, gestures, and sound to convey meanings. However, inside classrooms, students rarely have modes other than written text available to them to express their interpretations. If we make other modes available to students, they might explore and investigate their potential for representing and communicating ideas, thereby deepening their comprehension of literature.

Our Intentions: In this lesson we want to show readers how to utilize Powerpoint presentations to express their interpretations of literature. Students will be able to explore how sound, image, video, and text can allow them to respond to literature in different and unique ways.

Lesson Overview: Using the chapter book *Out of the Dust* by Karen Hesse (1997), students will construct a Powerpoint presentation that represents various interpretations of the text through a variety of modes. The lesson will begin with a whole-class demonstration of how to put various pieces of a presentation together and discuss how Powerpoint can be used to deepen their understandings of the text. Students will also analyze the potential of Powerpoint as a resource for response to literature.

Language of Instruction: Good morning, Readers! Today we are going to extend our responses to *Out of the Dust* by Karen Hesse as part of our Dust Bowl and Great Depression unit of study. I would like to share with you another tool for responding to literature that many of you are familiar with already: Powerpoint. To begin, when I say the word *mode*, what do you think about? [*Discuss.*] I think about still and moving images, gesture, sound, text, graphics, drama, sculpture, and talk. Those are what we call modes of expression. When we think about Powerpoint as a tool for response, think about all the things we can do with this tool. Let's take a look at some of the possibilities for using Powerpoint as a way of representing our ideas (see Figure 1.7).

Still Image	Video	Text	Sound
Drawing	Historic videos Documentaries	Text as caption	Voice in a movie or narration
Photos	Home videos of our interpretation	Report Description Any kind of writing	Sound effects and voice-over

FIG. 1.7 *Possibilities for Using Powerpoint*

May be copied for classroom use. © 2008 by Frank Serafini and Suzette Youngs, from *More (Advanced) Lessons in Comprehension*. Portsmouth, NH: Heinemann.

The chart shows us some of the things we can do with a Powerpoint presentation in response to literature. On our list we have image, video, text, and sound. Let's talk about what each mode can do for our responses to *Out of the Dust*.

In pairs, please choose one of the modes that you are interested in working with and in your reader-response notebook brainstorm how that mode might help you to respond to *Out of the Dust*. Each pair will create a response using that mode and then we will put it all together in one Powerpoint presentation. We will look at all of the parts and see how it can all be put together. Then we will analyze how each mode contributed something different to our overall understanding of the text.

Instructional Trajectory:

Once using Powerpoint and the various modes that can be incorporated in this tool has been modeled as a whole class, students feel braver about choosing less traditional responses to the books they read. They will be able to apply this type of response to anything they read as well as apply these experiences with this technology to other projects and presentations.

Classroom Artifacts:

Students created charts and Powerpoint presentations in response to *Out of the Dust*. Some features students planned to include in the Powerpoint: written text expressing opinions about the book and the literary elements they noticed; videos of dust storms or reenactment of an important scene; pictures or clip art to represent a theme; images from that historical period that portray the setting, the people, and what they endured; sound effects to capture the sound of the dust storms; or silence to show the main character's loneliness.

To give you a sense of this lesson's power and students' engagement, other students created a poem for two voices to convey Billie Jo and Pa's perspective; added drawings and captions of symbolic images (a cherry tree, tumbleweeds, piano, fire, and home); and wove in video clips of dust bowl storms with a voice-over of key passages, sounds of windstorms, and photo collages of various aspects of the Dust Bowl and Great Depression. Students found songs that were important for that historical period and analyzed the music and words, making robust connections to the book.

Closing Comments: Students utilized so many resources and modes of expression during this lesson to represent their understandings about the book and the Great Depression. These experiences aren't forgotten. They become part of the intellectual and practical repertoire students call on when they next analyze a piece of literature.

Expanding Interpretive Repertoires

The lessons in this strand were designed to help teachers expand students' interpretive repertoires—that is, their ability to approach texts and images from new theoretical and practical directions. These lessons, like all of the lessons in this book, should be considered signposts to guide students' journey toward comprehension and understanding; they're not the destination. In other words, the goal is not to get good at doing the intellectual exercises we describe in these lessons, the goal is to get better at generating interpretations and understandings in transactions with texts and images.

In this strand, we turn our attention to new ways of talking and thinking about picturebooks and other short texts that can be read and explored in one session. Each lesson offers suggestions for helping students generate initial impressions or interpretations, and provides opportunities for teachers and students to reflect on these initial interpretations. It is this blend of initial response and reflective thinking that is the hallmark of these lessons.

In conducting our workshops, we use the term *co-elaboration* to suggest the interactive nature of literary discussions, and that we must elaborate together on each other's thinking. The text is then a point of departure for students' myriad and sometimes messy interpretations and for our literary discussions, not the source of all meaning. We don't want the goal of these lessons and discussions to be reaching a consensus about a main idea or an interpretation, but instead want students to draw upon the text to infer, interpret, and perhaps diverge from peers with their thinking and the connections they are making.

High-quality discussions begin with high-quality literature. We have carefully selected the texts for these lessons to support the sophisticated discussions we hope will ensue. Our goal is to expand readers' interpretive abilities and perspectives through extended response strategies, the coding of texts during one's reading, and the construction of visual artifacts to support students' thinking and provide access to ideas previously offered.

The comprehension lessons in this section include:

2.1 What Is Noticed, What Is Known

2.2 Structured Coding: Speech Bubbles

2.3 Structured Coding: Four Prompts

What Is Noticed, What Is Known

The Challenge: Predicting has become a prominent activity in many lessons and reading strategy instruction. As one of the seven "featured" comprehension strategies, predicting has been used to build background knowledge, and help readers attend to the story being read or shared. However, there are times when the focus of readers' attention is on the predicting itself, and not on its use as a comprehension strategy. Too often, predicting becomes a guessing game about what is up ahead, or a search for who can make the best guesses, not as a strategy to get students to logically anticipate future events in a story. Making sense should take precedence over being able to guess what an author did.

Our Intentions: There are strategies beyond predicting to help build background knowledge before reading a text. In this comprehension lesson, we want to call students' attention to *what is in front of them*, not what is up ahead in the story. By asking them what they notice and what they know, rather than focusing on what they have not yet encountered, we can call readers' attention to the visual and textual components that readers draw upon to make sense as they read.

Lesson Overview: Using a picturebook by an author or illustrator readers are familiar with, we call readers' attention to the information that is available on the cover, endpages, and other opening materials as readers approach a text. This lesson is designed to help teachers introduce texts during a read-aloud or discussion without having to always begin by having students predict what might occur in the story. This lesson involves creating a list of words and ideas that readers offer as they approach a particular text.

Language of Instruction: Good morning, Readers! Often, before we read a story, and especially in school, we are asked what we think might happen. You might know this activity as *predicting*. Well, in today's lesson I want you to think about what you see or notice and what you know, not what you don't know. I am going to hold up this new book called *Probuditi* by one of our favorite authors and illustrators, Chris Van Allsburg (2006), and I want you to tell me something you notice or something you know. As you tell me things you notice and know, I will write some of your ideas on a chart so we can discuss these things when we are done. Let's begin by looking at the front cover of the book. So tell me, young readers, what do you notice or know? [*Students discuss.*] I see that you are commenting on both the visual images and the textual elements and I think that is great. There is more to talk about when we look at the front and back covers of a book than just the illustrations. We should consider the author, the title, and any text that is included. Some things I am always looking for when I approach a new book are things that are different, things that stand out, or things I have never seen before. Let's continue with what you are noticing.

Instructional Trajectory: Having students slow down and pay close attention to the covers, book jackets, end-pages, title pages, and other paratextual resources is an important strategy. We would like to see students begin discussing these resources and components in their literature response logs, and whole-class or small-group literature discussions. This strategy can be used with any text and allows readers to bring up anything that they noticed in both the visual or textual elements. In other words, it doesn't limit readers' attention to one particular aspect of reading or the text the way that predicting might.

Classroom Artifacts: The comments and responses offered by students will be used to construct a chart on Noticings/Knowings (Figure 2.1). The point of this chart is for readers to draw on these ideas as they approach similar texts throughout the year. This chart can serve as a foundation for other "approaching a text" strategies that are taught later.

Closing Comments: Helping teachers find things to do that get students' ideas flowing before they encounter a text is an important consideration. We believe that predicting what might happen before we read a book may not be the best way to accomplish this task. Predicting is about what is *not* known, while our strategy focuses on what resources are available to the reader and what *is* known before one begins reading.

FIG. 2.1 *What Is Noticed, Known Chart*—Voices in the Park

May be copied for classroom use. © 2008 by Frank Serafini and Suzette Youngs, from *More (Advanced) Lessons in Comprehension*. Portsmouth, NH: Heinemann.

Noticed	Known
There is a red hat on the ground on the back cover.	Anthony Browne uses monkeys as characters.
The letters in the title are all different fonts.	Browne writes weird books and includes weird things in his illustrations.
The front cover has two kids in a park.	The book is a sequel to a *Walk in the Park*.
It looks like autumn and summer on the front cover.	The book has four sections or voices.
The back cover has four sentence fragments all starting with *I*.	It will take us more than one reading to make sense of this book.

Structured Coding: Speech Bubbles

The Challenge: Since reading comprehension is an invisible process, understanding what readers are doing during the act of reading is far from an easy endeavor. Nevertheless, when we have students write, talk, draw, or "code" texts we can gain insight into what they are thinking about. As teachers, our challenge is to gain these insights without interrupting the flow of the students' reading.

Our Intentions: In this lesson, we have students *code* texts—highlighting, writing notes, placing sticky notes on sections or pages of a book—all with an eye to helping them return to the text to review what they have been thinking and comprehending. These codes also become effective assessment tools, providing clues to what a reader feels is important for understanding as they read. What readers attend to and what they overlook can provide insights into their thinking and comprehension processes.

Lesson Overview: Readers will read a selected picturebook and place sticky notes shaped like speech bubbles on illustrations and textural components to indicate what they think is occurring and what they are inferring about a character's thinking. These coded texts can be used as a thinking and talking device for extending classroom discussions and interpretations.

Language of Instruction: Good morning, Readers! Today I am going to share with you a new type of sticky note. Take a look at these stickies! These are shaped like the speech bubbles we often see in comic books and cartoons. When an artist or author places these above a character's head it is usually to show what a character is saying or thinking. I found some of these speech bubble stickies at an office supply store and was thinking that they might work well in our reading workshop. We could use them to write down what we think a particular character is saying or what they might be thinking. I am going to demonstrate what I mean by this and then we try it as a group. So let's take a look at one of our favorite picturebooks, *The Three Pigs* by David Weisner (2001). Take a look at the page that I have marked. On this page I wrote that the wolf was confused and was wondering what happened to the pig when he huffed and puffed and blew the house in. It looks to me as though he doesn't understand where the pig went. So, I took one of these speech bubble stickies and wrote about the wolf being confused and placed it above the wolf's head. Let's turn to a different page and see if you can think of some ideas to put on a speech bubble of your own.

Instructional Trajectory: This lesson is not an invitation to fill up books with sticky notes! Like any instructional technique, use it strategically rather than overuse it. The point of the lesson is to get readers to infer ideas from the text and their lived experiences. The value of the lesson will be evident in reader-response notebooks and discussions when they begin to discuss character motives and thoughts that are not directly stated in the text.

Classroom Artifacts: These experiences do not lend themselves to charts as much as they produce books that contain a variety of sticky notes. One possibility is to take the speech bubbles out of the texts and organize them into categories. It may be interesting to see any patterns that arise when doing this across particular texts, characters, genres, or authors. It can also be interesting to read aloud a book that still has the sticky note comments of other readers. After the read-aloud, let the class read the comments of other readers. This history of other readers' interpretations can then be used to extend classroom discussions and responses to the discussion.

Closing Comments: This comprehension lesson works well with more challenging picturebooks that have complex plot lines, characters, and possibilities for constructing interpretations. Be sure to choose a picturebook that has an interesting main character, and plenty of opportunities for filling in gaps in the story.

Structured Coding: Four Prompts

The Challenge: In the same way that we used speech bubble codes to direct students to attend to characters' motives, understandings, and actions (see Lesson 2.2), this lesson directs students to attend to four particular aspects of the text or illustrations. Perception is a motivated process, meaning we learn through experience to attend to certain things and not others. In this structured coding experience, students focus on certain aspects of a story, and consider things they may not have perceived or attended to on their own.

Our Intentions: We want to make students aware of particular aspects of a story or a visual image so that they are on the lookout for them in all their future reading. In a sense we are training their eyes to "notice" more and more as they read—and to notice some key aspects of text and visual cues. We accomplish this by asking students to answer teacher-generated questions on four separate sticky notes. These notes are then used as a vehicle for extending discussions by noting both students' common answers and unique interpretations.

Lesson Overview: Students will be given four sticky notes and asked to respond to the following four questions:

1. What is something you expected in the story?
2. What is something missing from the story or illustrations?
3. What surprised you in the story or illustrations?
4. How did the character change during the story?

Language of Instruction: Good morning, Readers! We have been using sticky notes to generate ideas in the novels we have read and some of the picturebooks we have shared. Today, I am going to ask you to focus on four different things as we read our story (see list above). Some of the things on this list are aspects of stories we have considered before, and a couple of them may be new. I would like you to listen carefully as I read today's story, *The Straight Line Wonder* by Mem Fox (1997), and make some notes on the four stickies that I have provided on your clipboards. When we are done with the story, I will give you some time to finish your thoughts. Then, we will display these notes on our class chart and reflect on our ideas and interpretations. What comes to your mind as I read is what is important, not what someone else is writing about. There are many interesting things in this book that are worth considering. Try to have something written down on each of these stickies.

Instructional Trajectory: We would assume that the prompts or questions that are asked for this lesson will become talking points used in literary discussions in the future. The prompts or questions generated by the teacher should help students move beyond the literal story itself and construct interpretations based on their experiences. The aspects of text and illustrations we call students' attention to in our whole-group discussions signify to students what is important and worth considering as they read. The questions should have a particular focus, but not to the point of excluding other possible aspects worth considering. It may be worthwhile to include a miscellaneous category to allow room for students' ideas that don't fit in the four sticky notes.

Classroom Artifacts: A cumulative class chart that includes students' individual notes for each of the four prompts will be generated and used for discussion.

Closing Comments: There is nothing magical about the number four or the prompts in this example. Consider what has been going on in your own discussions and use the sticky notes to call students' attention to aspects of the text and illustrations your students have not been attending to.

❖ What is something you noticed?

❖ How was the story structured?

❖ Did the design (endpages, format, covers) add to the story?

❖ What questions do you have?

❖ What artistic style was used by the illustrator?

❖ Was there any special language or words in the text that caught your attention?

❖ How did the title relate to the story?

FIG. 2.2 *Additional Questions for Structured Coding*

Moving Beyond the Literal

The Challenge: In many traditional classrooms, the questions teachers ask, and the goal of many litera-ture discussions, is to attend to all that is factual or literal in the text. Students are asked to comment on the plot, describe the characters, notice details in the illustrations, and other literal elements during discussions. This is going to take our readers only so far. We need to provide opportunities and support for students to move beyond the literal text, to construct inferences and deeper interpretations about what's going on between char-acters if we are going to fully support students' comprehension processes.

Our Intentions: Utilizing an adapted version of a Noticings, Connections, Wonderings chart (see Serafini 2001 for original chart), our goal is to help students take what they notice and work to interpret what these things might mean. The literal elements are used as a "point of de-parture" for students' interpretive processes.

Lesson Overview: Using a selected a picturebook, poem, or short text, students will be asked to participate in constructing a three-column chart. This chart (see Figure 2.3) will be a tool for en-riching discussions. It will also demonstrate to readers that the literal text is useful to lay the groundwork at the beginning of a discussion, but that reading and discussing books is most satisfying when we read between the lines of a text, making meaning with a far bigger repertoire of interpretive instruments.

Language of Instruction: Good morning, Readers! Today we are going to read a wonderful picturebook called *Into the Forest* by one of our favorite authors, Anthony Browne (2004). Like all of the books by Anthony Browne we have read before, this one will probably have some unusual elements. Can anyone tell me a few things we might encounter in one of Browne's picturebooks? [*Discussion*] Great! You will notice on the wall behind me that we have a new type of chart. This one is similar to our Noticings, Connections, Wonderings chart, but it is also different. Let's take a look at the three headings. The first heading, What We Noticed, is the same as our other charts. In this column, we want to pay attention to de-tails in the written text, the design, the extra-textual materials (endpages, title page, and so on), and the illustrations and discuss what we notice. However, the second and third columns are different. In the second column, I want you to talk about those things that you noticed in the first column, and then offer an interpretation or idea about what it might mean. This is the most important part of reading: thinking about what you have noticed and what it might mean. The third column sounds kind of like a smart aleck, but not really. What I want you to talk about in that column are the possible implications or future ramifications of our interpretations. Let me explain. If we noticed that there is a girl with a little red coat in the story (which there actually is in this book), we might

What We Noticed	What This Might Mean	So What
The book looks small in the illustrations.	Browne is making us think the forest is big and scary.	Fairy tales are writt... children to listen to their parents.
Most of the illustrations are black and white.	This looks like an old, classic black-and-white movie.	It is supposed to be an old traditional story.
The girl's red coat stands out in the illustrations.	She is supposed to be Little Red Riding Hood.	Browne is using other fairy tales to get us to relate to this new story.
There are things from other fairy tales hidden in the forest.	All fairy tales are connected.	We use other stories to understand the ones we are reading.

notice the coat and the color first. Then, we might suggest that this coat is the same as Little Red Riding Hood and relates to that fairy tale. The So What? part comes in when you say that Anthony Browne uses connections to other fairy tales in many of his stories and we may consider what this suggests for reading this story and any other stories by him. Do you have any questions about this new chart? OK, let's give it a try.

Instructional Trajectory: Using the literal text and illustrations as a point of departure for our discussions supports students as they develop their thinking beyond literal recall. They learn to draw inferences and to use these inferences to construct nuanced interpretations that radiate across stories and experiences. We should recognize and celebrate these types of responses and interpretations during our discussions and as we read students' reader-response notebooks. Guiding our students as they make the shift from the literal to the literary is the basis of our reading workshop philosophy, a philosophy founded on the notion that we have to change the way we think and talk about texts in our schools.

Classroom Artifacts: The new three-column chart will be the primary artifact.

Closing Comments: Asking students to notice more than what is obvious in a text and illustrations, and to consider what these elements might mean can be challenging. Many of our students come to us from classrooms that privilege literal questions and noticings. Although we believe that perception is the initial impetus that begins the interpretive process, it does students a disservice to let them remain at the literal level. Until they can discuss what things mean, we'd be hard pressed to call them proficient, let alone critical readers. Students get this, too, and they rise to the challenge, though it won't happen overnight. They like that their insights and interpretations matter, and respect that we are setting new expectations for them. With this lesson and all others, we are demonstrating that reading is a thinking process, not simply about oral proficiency and memory.

Paratextual Resources

The Challenge: All books, to some extent, come with extra-textual materials used to introduce the story, author, and illustrator; promote sales of the book; pique readers' interests; offer additional information about the author or background of the story; and prepare the reader for the upcoming story. Too often, novice readers overlook these materials. Without considering the larger contexts in which books are situated, and the paratextual materials that are available both within and outside the covers of a book, readers enter the story at a disadvantage compared with those who slow down when approaching a text and consider all of these elements.

Our Intentions: We intend to call students' attention to the variety of materials that are made available for a single picturebook or novel. We first encountered the terms *peritext*, *epitext*, and *paratextual materials* during our discussions with Dr. Larry Sipe. He introduced us to the work of a French literary theorist named Gerard Genette. Genette uses the word *paratextual* as the overall term for both peritextual materials (things included *in* the book but not directly part of the story like endpages, dedications, author blurbs) and epitextual materials (things that are outside the text like advertisements, websites, posters, book reviews). Both peritextual and epitextual materials can be used to extend readers' interpretive focus by relating the story to those things that accompany its publication.

Lesson Overview: By collecting a variety of epitextual materials that pertain to a particular book, we help students make connections among the actual story, the author's experiences, and the design elements and promotional materials made available by publishers. In addition, we cannot forget that children's literature is an economic commodity that is bought and sold, and because of this, picturebooks come with all the accoutrements of a commercial product.

Language of Instruction: Good morning, Readers! I am going to introduce you to two new words today. They are called *peritextual* and *epitextual*. I'm sure you have never heard of these two words, but I am also sure you will understand what they mean right away. *Peritextual* means all of the things that are included in a book that aren't part of the story. These elements are usually created by the publisher, but some are made by the author or illustrator. We have noticed and discussed many of these things every time we have shared a new book. The peritext includes things like the dedication, the endpages, and the book jacket information. Now we have a word for all of this stuff. *Epitextual* is a bit different. It refers to all of the stuff about a book that is outside it. Can you think of any things that might come with a book that aren't actually inside it? [*Discussion*] That's right. Things like advertisements, authors' websites, book reviews, and sometimes toys and games. We can learn a lot about a particular book before we even open it up if we consider both the peritextual and epitextual materials that are associated with a book. I have located a website of one of our favorite authors, Kevin Henkes (www.kevinhenkes.com). Let's take a look at his website and a couple of interviews I found and consider what is being offered.

Instructional Trajectory: Evidence of this lesson's effectiveness will be found by observing how readers approach texts in the future. We want students to slow down as they approach a text and consider both materials included in the actual book and made available in reviews, websites, and commercial materials. The more we can situate the particular book we are reading, the better we can understand what the implications are for a particular story.

Classroom Artifacts: Teachers and students may collect materials on particular books or authors and illustrators in binders to display in their classroom libraries. These collections of epitextual materials can be revisited by students for further information or to generate ideas for new books to read or authors and illustrators to explore.

Closing Comments: Contemporary picturebooks are utilizing the paratextual space to add clues to enhance the story and information that extends the possibilities of the book's design. Students tend to bypass all these materials, viewing them as extraneous to the story. As authors and illustrators continue to play with the borders of books, we need to call students' attention to what is being made available for experiencing the picturebook—or any book—to its fullest.

Insider–Outsider Perspectives with Picturebooks

The Challenge: Whether we recognize them or not, every text includes the perspectives and sociocultural understandings of its authors and illustrators. The characters and stories created by the author and illustrator privilege certain points of view and marginalize others. It is important to understand when readers can connect with the characters or events in a story, and when these experiences don't align with the way they view the world. Being able to read as an *insider*, or when the experiences of the character in the story matches with the reader's experiences, is much easier than reading as an *outsider*, or when these experiences don't align. We can help readers recognize these two perspectives and provide strategies for each stance.

Our Intentions: We want students to become more capable of discussing books that portray experiences they themselves have not previously encountered. Authors write about things readers have not experienced firsthand, people we have not met, and places and times we have not traveled. One's lack of experience should not prevent readers from comprehending and enjoying a story. By acknowledging that one has not "walked in the characters' shoes," readers are able to discuss how the character might feel, but most important to admit their lack of understanding of a situation. This admission opens avenues for new discussions.

Lesson Overview: This lesson will focus on two picturebooks, one that has been selected because of familiar characters and situations and one that focuses on circumstances that don't align with our students' experiences. By discussing how readers react and interact with each book, discussions can focus on both insider and outsider perspectives.

Language of Instruction: Good morning, Readers! Today we are going to discuss what I call "insider" and "outsider" perspectives. Let me explain the difference. When you are reading a book and you can relate to a character, you understand what they are going through, or you have been through the same experiences yourself, I would call that an insider perspective. When you are reading a book and you are having a hard time relating to or understanding what is happening to the characters because you have never experienced something like that or have never been to the setting of the story, I would call that an outsider perspective. Sometimes you can feel both ways in a single book, where there are events in the story you can closely relate to, and other events that you haven't experienced. Let me see if these two books can explain more about what I am thinking. I am sure that most of us at one time or another have gotten angry. Am I right? Of course. In the book *When*

Sophie Gets Angry—Really, Really Angry . . . the author Molly Bang (1999) describes what it is like sometimes to get angry and some good ways to deal with your anger. I'm sure that we can all relate to that, right?

In the second book, *Hooway for Wodney Wat* by Helen Lester (1999), the character has a speech problem and gets picked on by the rest of the class. Most of you don't have a noticeable speech problem, but some of you may have been picked on for something else. Depending on your experiences, you may feel like an insider or an outsider when you read this book. These two perspectives mean that we relate to a book differently. Sometimes it seems easier to relate to a book if you have had the same experiences as the main character. That's fine. But sometimes it's important to get a sense of what it is like to be someone else. The outsider perspective can help us understand and empathize with other points of view. I think both of these perspectives are important. I have collected several books here that I think will force many of you to experience both perspectives. Let's break into groups of two or three and read one of these books and keep a list of the times during the reading where you felt like an insider or an outsider. Then, we can come back together and discuss what we think.

Instructional Trajectory: We would like to see readers acknowledging their perspectives in future discussions and in their reader-response notebooks. Empathy and making personal connections both coincide with an insider perspective. Outsider perspectives are more difficult to work with, but can be used to broaden students' perceptions of the world.

Classroom Artifacts: Classroom charts focusing on why particular students felt like an insider or outsider at certain points in the story would support these discussions.

Closing Comments: Children's literature has been metaphorically compared with a "window on the world" and a "mirror unto oneself." This lesson focuses on both the window and mirror metaphors, supporting students' understandings and discussions concerning topics that they themselves may not have experienced, and those that provide a mirror on their own experiences. Although classroom teachers should ensure that many of the titles in their classroom libraries directly relate to the lives of the students in their classes, it is equally important to introduce students to new perspectives, experiences, people, and places. Reading historical fiction, for example, can be challenging because readers are forced into an outsider perspective, and bring a limited amount of background knowledge to these stories.

Book Scene Investigation (BSI)

The Challenge: Comparing and contrasting two stories, or characters, settings, and other literary elements, has been considered a traditional reading skill, one that is included on most standardized tests. Often, this is seen as some isolated skill that students have to master if they are to be considered a proficient reader. However, in real life students compare and contrast things all the time. It is actually called evaluating or passing judgments. Give a student two books and ask them which one they enjoyed the most and they usually have no trouble giving you an answer. They might have trouble explaining their answer, or understanding how to compare and contrast items on a standardized test. This is where the challenge lies.

Our Intentions: We certainly want readers to offer their opinions as freely as possible in our literature discussions. Aidan Chambers calls this type of response "honorably reported." While freely offering one's opinion is an important starting point, being able to defend one's interpretations is equally as important.

Lesson Overview: Drawing on students' experiences with television crime dramas, like *CSI: Crime Scene Investigation*, we will discuss how we provide evidence of our interpretations, and how we can construct warranted evaluations and interpretations of what we read.

Language of Instruction: Good morning, Readers! How many of you have ever watched *CSI, NYPD Blue, Law and Order*, or any other police dramas? [*Brief discussion*] OK, did you ever notice how the police depend on evidence to make their case, and the prosecuting attorney has to have enough evidence to take a case to trial? Well, I think it is the same thing in interpreting literature. When we get an idea about a book, it should be based on some evidence. This evidence can come from the book, our experiences, or other books we have read. But there should be some reason why we think certain things. Have you noticed how many times during our discussions that I have said, "Could you tell me more about that idea?" Well, what I am trying to do is to get you to explain your thinking. I want you to explain why you came to the interpretation or conclusion that you made, and to provide evidence of your interpretation. When I ask you that question, it's not because I think you're wrong, it's because I am *really* interested in what you think and why you think certain things. So, don't be intimidated when I ask for more of your ideas. We have to get our ideas out on the table if we are going to discuss and evaluate them. I expect you to be able to provide evidence of your thinking and be able to share your interpretations, and I expect you to share how you came to those interpretations. This is going to be challenging at first, but it is the most important aspect of our discussions. We need to be able to explain our thinking so we can get more sophisticated in our interpretations of what we read.

Instructional Trajectory: When we start to see readers using the word *because* in their reader-response notebooks, it usually signals they are providing evidence for their interpretations, or at least how they arrived at their conclusions. We may write questions in reader-response notebooks asking them to explain why they made the interpretations they did. These questions are not intended to intimidate readers, but to demonstrate that providing evidence of one's thinking is an important aspect of our reading workshop.

Classroom Artifacts: Using artifacts similar to crime scene photos and courtroom evidence, we expect readers to be able to provide links among their interpretations, the text, and the world. Many of the artifacts for these lessons will come from the text itself, but others may come from biographies, authors' and illustrators' websites, book blurbs and jackets, and commercial advertisements.

Closing Comments: We tend to make discussions literary "hot seats." This is an important lesson, but one that will be supported more by the way we respond to students than the types of questions we ask. We can tell students to share their ideas honestly because we really care about what they think, but if we don't listen sensitively and honestly to what they say, or we dismiss their ideas outright, it won't take long for students to realize that we are just giving lip service to their interpretations.

Dual Storyboards

The Challenge: Novice readers typically have difficulty seeing the overall structure of a story, picture-book, or novel. One of the ways this difficulty presents itself is how hard it is for some students to write a summary of a story. What is usually provided by students when asked to summarize a story is some form of plot-based flowchart, where students simply retell the events that took place sequentially. In order to write a summary, readers need to see the overall structure of the story, as well as its themes and major implications. In order to summarize, one has to think about the big picture.

Our Intentions: To help readers see the big picture of a story, Frank described how he "storyboarded" the picturebook *Where the Wild Things Are* (Sendak 1963) in his book *The Reading Workshop: Creating Space for Readers* (Serafini 2001). One of the wonderful classroom teachers we have worked with, Staca Sadie, took Frank's idea of storyboarding and created a *parallel storyboard*. She displayed the books *Jumanji* (1981) and *Zathura* (2002), both by Chris Van Allsburg, in parallel fashion, one above the other, on her classroom wall. These two stories related to each other, and the storyboard was designed to help students make connections across the texts and illustrations of these books.

Lesson Overview: By presenting the parallel storyboard display of *Jumanji* and *Zathura*, we will illuminate for students how stories have similar structures and how authors and illustrators may use the same techniques and literary devices in the books they create. Both books are displayed across the classroom wall so that children can simultaneously view the illustrations and text, and can compare the two story structures.

Language of Instruction: Good morning, Readers! Remember when I put the illustrations of *Where the Wild Things Are* up across the room? Well, as you probably noticed when you came in this morning, I have displayed two of Chris Van Allsburg's books we have been reading on the back wall of the classroom. This time, I put one book above the other to give us a chance to compare the two stories and illustrations. Let's take a quick look and see what we notice first. [*Provide time to observe and discuss the storyboards.*] OK, let's come back together and talk about what we noticed. I want to be sure we take a look at how similar the two stories are, and also how the two books differ. For example, both books begin with a game that presents a problem for the characters. Both books explore in detail the challenges the characters undergo, and both books solve the problem at the end, but in different ways. We can look at specific details, like the points of view of the illustrations, the media and artistic choices and the words Van Allsburg uses, or we can look at the overall structure of the two books. Of course, we could do this with other books as well.

Can anyone think of two books that might be interesting to compare to one another? Let's construct a Noticings, Connections, Wonderings chart for these two books and see what looking at the two books at the same time does for our discussions.

Instructional Trajectory: There are several ways that this lesson can support readers into the future. Helping readers discuss the "gist" of a story and summarize the points they feel are important is a valuable practice that can support more sophisticated discussions and response notebook entries. Being able to compare and contrast two works by an author is an a vital skill to develop. Finally, attending to the visual as well as textual elements of a story is important for moving beyond literal meanings to interpretations and critique.

Classroom Artifacts: We like putting storyboards up on the classroom wall with butcher paper underneath to provide space for our commentaries and noticings. The notes on the paper can be used to stimulate discussions and charted by themselves.

Closing Comments: The point in this lesson is not to make nice decorations on the wall, though these books are interesting when you can view them in their entirety. The goal is to discuss the structures of stories and to help students see overarching similarities and differences in stories. We don't want to get bogged down in the specific details of illustrations and story all the time. There is a time and place for scavenger hunts, and there is a time and place for attending to the big picture.

Reconsidering Teacher Talk and Classroom Interactions

The ways in which we talk with students, the actual language of classroom interactions and instruction, play an important role in the quality of the reading lessons we provide. Traditionally, classroom teachers interact with students in a pattern that has been referred to as the *Initiate–Respond–Evaluate* (IRE) interaction pattern. This has also been called a *recitation script*, because students are simply expected to recite and recall what has been asked for or prompted by the teacher. In these IRE interactions, the teacher dominates the discussion, taking turns at will and allocating turns to others, determining appropriate topics and comments, and endorsing particular answers and interpretations.

This pattern has tremendous appeal because of its long history in education, the control it offers teachers, the perceived need to cover the curriculum, and the many models of teaching that teachers have observed throughout their careers that support this traditional way of interacting with students. Breaking this interaction pattern takes conscious attention on the part of the teacher, and the willingness to relinquish some control of the discussions and interpretations to students.

In contrast to the IRE pattern, a two-way, transactional discourse or interaction pattern invites students to contribute more substantially to the discussions, provides opportunities for students to ask their own questions and pose topics, opens up turn taking, and focuses on a diversity of ideas rather than a search for the one main idea presumed hidden in the text. These "interactive" discussions are two-way exchanges, opening space for students' interpretations and opinions. The primary quality of these discussions is their "interactivity," measured by how much students are involved in the discussion. The goal is to get everyone talking to and listening to one another, not simply speaking at each other through the teacher.

Language is used as a bridge from what is known to what is being learned. We use language to regulate the complexity of the tasks we require students to complete, in this case discussing and interpreting a particular text. Classroom teachers use language as a scaffold for their lessons, paying attention to when students seem confused, and offering additional support when this occurs. The primary goal of the lessons included in this strand is to get students to expand their interpretations and responses, generating, articulating, and negotiating meaning in a community of readers.

Focusing on the language of instruction and discussion seems the next logical step in the trajectory we have set for our academic writings. We have tried to articulate our preferred vision for the reading workshop, then focused more closely on the lessons in comprehension, now in this strand we focus on the actual language of the lessons and discussions we hope to establish.

The comprehension lessons in this section include:

3.1 Setting Expectations for Discussions

3.2 Literary Discussion Goldfish Bowl

3.3 Platforming: Putting Ideas on the Table

3.4 Uptake: Taking Up from What Has Been Offered

3.5 Display, Procedural, Process, and Inquiry Questions

3.6 He Said, She Said, I Think

3.7 Critical Junctures

3.8 Dialogue Blockers

Setting Expectations for Discussion

The Challenge: In order to foster more sophisticated discussions that focus on literature and informational texts, we need to be sure that students aren't just talking past one another without listening to what has been shared. Offering ideas for other students to consider, listening attentively when another student is speaking, and negotiating meanings and interpretations are important aspects of a sophisticated literary discussion. We cannot assume that students will naturally become active listeners and contributors to our literary discussions. We need to set clear expectations for what we expect readers to work toward in our classroom discussions.

Our Intentions: We want to be sure that students understand the objectives and procedures for classroom discussions. By setting clear, transparent, obtainable expectations, teachers encourage students to participate in discussions. We want students to work together during literature discussions to elaborate on what has been offered and consider the possibilities for what has been discussed. It is an active stance toward discussions, opening up possibilities for new interpretations, rather than trying to reach agreement and consensus.

Lesson Overview: By sharing a story about listening and the perils of not paying attention, we help students understand the importance of attending to others' contributions, and create a chart outlining the expectations for subsequent literature discussions.

Language of Instruction: Good morning, Listeners! That's right, I said "listeners" instead of "readers" this morning. I did that because today we are going to talk about the importance of listening attentively to one another during our literature discussions. Let me start by reading a book called *Listen Buddy* by Helen Lester (1995). [*Read and discuss book.*] There were some interesting consequences of Buddy not listening in that story weren't there? Let's take a look at the chart I have created on the wall behind me (see Figure 3.1). The most important characteristic of a good discussion isn't how many people talk, but how many people listen.

Have you ever pretended to listen to your parents when they were talking to you, but really your mind has left the building? Yeah, me too. But that type of listening doesn't support the type of discussions we are trying to have in our classroom. We need to really listen and attend to what each of us is saying if we are going to learn from each other. Let's try a few things to get started. Let's arrange ourselves in a circle so we can see each other, and when someone is talking be sure to look at that person to show you respect

FIG. 3.1
Setting Expectations for Discussions

1. Honest Reporting—say what you really think

2. Listening and Thinking Is as Important as Talking—we all like to be heard

3. Address Other Students as Well as the Teacher—look at them, and face them when you are talking or listening

4. Half-Baked Ideas Are Accepted and Encouraged—no "final ideas" are needed, thinking and interpretation is a process

5. Consider What Has Been Offered—where does this fit in your thinking?

6. Respect Differences of Opinion—consensus is NOT the goal, but seeing new possibilities

what they are saying. When we look directly at someone we have a better chance of hearing what they are saying. I'm not saying that you can't listen and look at the floor, but sometimes our minds wander and we forget to pay attention. So today, let's try to look at one another when someone is speaking and talk some more about Buddy and what happened to him in the story, and consider the other items I have included on our class chart.

Instructional Trajectory: As the school year progresses, we expect our discussions to get richer and more sophisticated. It is important to understand that the teacher is the primary model for demonstrating "active listening." If the teacher does not demonstrate how to sit and listen well, chances are the students won't become active listeners either. If as teachers we don't listen closely to what students are saying, why would we expect students to listen closely? Changing interaction patterns takes time and patience. Students have been socialized into a particular way of acting in classrooms and our goal is to change that pattern of interaction.

Classroom Artifacts: The chart offered here is a sample of some of the expectations that we encourage students to adopt.

Closing Comments: The idea of honesty in discussions, or "honorably reported" responses, came from Aidan Chambers in his book *Tell Me: Children, Reading, and Talk* (1996). If students do not tell us what they are really thinking, we will never move past banal conversations into more sophisticated dialogue. Dialogue requires intellectual and emotional investment. It is a passionate form of discussion where students share interpretations and negotiate meanings and ideas that are important to them. Setting clear and obtainable expectations for discussions from the beginning of the year is an important ritual to establish.

Literary Discussion Goldfish Bowl

The Challenge: Many students have been asked to participate in literature discussions, but many have never seen a quality literature discussion take place. In order to really learn how to do something, it is important to read and talk about it, but equally important to actually watch it take place and listen to the way participants respond to one another.

Our Intentions: By conducting a literature discussion among several teachers or adults in front of a group of students, we can demonstrate the ways participants offer ideas, wait for opportunities to speak, listen attentively to one another, take up from one another's interpretations, and negotiate meaning in a respectful, yet authentic manner.

Lesson Overview: In this lesson, several adults, including classroom teachers, gather together to discuss a selected piece of literature. The goal is to demonstrate a quality literature discussion while students play the role of "researchers" and take notes on what the participants said and did in order to discuss what occurred and how each member contributed to the discussion.

Language of Instruction: Good morning, Researchers! Yes, that's right, I said "researchers." Today, you are going to pay close attention to a literature discussion and take notes like researchers and scientists do about what you see happening. We are doing this because I want you to pay attention to what a quality discussion looks and sounds like so we can try and have some better discussions ourselves. As you can see I have asked a few parents and teachers to join me here today to talk about a book by one of our favorite authors, Natalie Babbitt. The book is called *Bub, or The Very Best Thing* (1994). We have not read this book yet this year, but don't worry, we will later this week. First, I want you to take out your reader-response notebooks and a pen so you can take notes about what you see us do and say during our discussion. We are going to begin with some general comments about the book and then we are going to talk about specific ideas we shared. I had each of the adults read the book before coming here today and take notes, much like you do, in a reader-response notebook. We will use our notes to add to our discussion. [*Discussion*]

Instructional Trajectory: Like the other lessons in this strand, the effects of this lesson will be seen in the quality of the discussions that occur as the year progresses. We don't expect the level of our discourse to change overnight, but we do expect students to attend to what we say and enact the strategies and procedures we teach them. It takes time to change the way students talk about texts. Students carry a lot of baggage from traditional classroom discussions and these don't disappear immediately.

Classroom Artifacts: Using students' notes and observations, the teacher will construct a T-chart (see Figure 3.2) listing things that help discussions on one side, and things that hinder discussions on the other. This list should be posted where students can refer to it during discussions. This chart can be revised and revisited as the year progresses. (See also Lesson 3.8 for a more extensive discussion on Dialogue Blockers.)

Closing Comments: Literature discussions grow more sophisticated as students' interpretive repertoires expand. It is important in this lesson to allow students to offer their ideas about what helped and hindered the discussion before offering the ideas in Lesson 3.8. We want students to know that the ideas they generate are as important as the ones we provide.

Helpers	Blockers

FIG. 3.2 *Dialogue Helpers and Blockers*

May be copied for classroom use. © 2008 by Frank Serafini and Suzette Youngs, from *More (Advanced) Lessons in Comprehension*. Portsmouth, NH: Heinemann.

Platforming: Putting Ideas on the Table

The Challenge: Some discussions seem to wander around from topic to topic and make it difficult for everyone to remember what has been said. As teachers pay close attention to what has been offered by students, it is their role to organize thoughts and offer summaries from time to time so students have a better sense of what the discussion is about, and where it is headed. Pulling ideas together is a primary role of a discussion facilitator.

Our Intentions: The idea of *platforming* is similar to recapping or summarizing during a discussion. Simply put, the teacher keeps track of where the discussion has been and from time to time synthesizes information and "puts it on the table" so students can consider what has been offered. Participants use this "platform" as a foundation for subsequent discussion.

Lesson Overview: During a literature discussion focusing on a particular text in a unit of study—an author study, for example—the teacher will pause during the discussion to summarize the ideas so far, chart some important thoughts, and prepare students to move forward in the discussion.

Language of Instruction: Good morning, Readers! I know that for the past week we have been reading books by one of our favorite authors, Graeme Base. Today's book is called *The Discovery of Dragons* (1996). We are going to spend a couple of days reading this book because it is much longer than some of the other picturebooks we have read by him. Before we begin, let's consider what we have learned so far about Graeme Base. [*Teacher shares a chart about ideas focusing on the books by Graeme Base read so far.*] As we begin to read *The Discovery of Dragons*, you will notice that Graeme refers to himself as Rowland W. Greasebeam, the author of this book. This is rather unusual, wouldn't you say? [*Discussion*] Let me read a few pages of the introduction to see where the book is headed. OK, let's stop for a minute and see what we have going on so far. We wrote on our author chart that Graeme Base typically uses four-stanza rhyme schemes in his book. Well, not in this one right? What else is different about this book? [*Discussion*] Also, so far in the book, we see many other characters being referred to but not present in the illustrations. In fact, there are no people as characters in the illustrations. That is rather unusual. Before we read any further, are there any other things we should mention?

Instructional Trajectory: The ability to summarize depends on one's ability to see the big picture of a text. Otherwise, students simply offer a series of events or plot episodes and call it summarizing. One way to help students learn to summarize is by demonstrating it frequently in authentic contexts in literature discussions. Platforming is a way that teachers can use summary to propel discussions forward by helping students see where the discussion has been. I believe students will start doing this in their literature study groups if prompted at the beginning and end of each discussion session.

Classroom Artifacts: Platforming can be done verbally or with a chart. In this lesson, the author chart was used to anchor the day's literature discussion, and verbal summary was used within the discussion to call students' attention to what had been offered.

Closing Comments: When you are reading a novel aloud each day to your class, you have to begin each session with a recap of the events that have preceded the new reading. This is the essence of platforming: stating where the discussion has been in order to make sense of what is coming up. We need to know where we have been if we are going to make sense of where we are going.

Uptake: Taking Up from What Has Been Offered

The Challenge: In traditional classroom interactions, teachers ask questions, lots of questions, and students are expected to provide answers. This pattern has been referred to as Initiate–Respond–Evaluate (IRE) by numerous researchers and educational theorists. In this type of interaction, teachers *Initiate* the discussion, usually by asking a question, students *Respond* to the question, and teachers *Evaluate* what has been offered by the student. This pattern has been shown to reduce the participation of students to one-word answers and does not support the interactivity that this strand of lessons is trying to establish and support.

Our Intentions: This lesson describes a different type of interaction pattern that disrupts the traditional IRE pattern. The goal of *uptake* is to *take up* from what students have said and help them reconsider what they offered, often leading them to clarify or extend their interpretations and comments (Nystrand 1997).

Lesson Overview: Using any picturebook, poem, or short text, this lesson focuses on the language used by teachers to respond to students' interpretations during literature discussions. The discussion described in Figure 3.3 is a revised transcript from an actual classroom literary discussion. In order to demonstrate how uptake works, we have decided to focus on a lesson we observed rather than describe in detail a lesson that we might use.

Lesson Transcript: This discussion, focusing on Anthony Browne's picturebook *Voices in the Park* (2001), took place in Suzette's intermediate grade classroom. Pay close attention to the way she listened to what students offered and how she used the students' comments to take up from what was said.

Instructional Trajectory: You will notice in this transcript that Suzette constantly refers to what has been offered by her students. Each subsequent comment demonstrates that she has listened to the students and is using their ideas as content for her responses. By taking up from what students say and offering suggestions, challenges, and opinions back to them, students learn that discussing is an active process of generating and negotiating meanings. It is our hope that these types of interactions will affect every discussion taking place in the classroom as students attend to what has been offered and speak back to what other students think.

Classroom Artifacts: none

Closing Comments: Uptake begins with teachers paying close attention to what students are saying. Too often, teachers simply praise students or paraphrase what students have said. Uptake requires teachers to attend to what is being discussed and to know enough about the piece of literature to challenge students to go deeper in their interpretations and discussions.

FIG. 3.3 Voices in the Park *Transcript*

> **Student:** I think the flower symbolizes how life is good and the daughter is happy. You know, friends and happiness.
>
> **Student:** It kind of has some hope.
>
> **Teacher:** It kind of gives you hope, doesn't it? These two kids are in a different generation, but they can change. Maybe with your generation you guys can get rid of prejudice and judgment and things like that. People are who they are. Maybe this is a sign of things to come.
>
> **Student:** On the very first page when they're walking together, they're not very happy and mom just has a straight face.
>
> **Student:** And then when the mom and Charles are sitting on the bench, they're kind of turned away from each other, they don't want to talk. And then again, down here, they're not looking at each other, talking or hugging or anything.
>
> **Student:** Then the last picture, the second to the last picture, she has her arm around him. But that's probably just, come on, we're not going back there.
>
> **Teacher:** So, you are getting the idea that Charles and his mother are very removed from each other. OK.
>
> **Student:** On this page, I noticed that she doesn't have a husband. Maybe because she's lost and looking for Charles and it only mentions two people in her family so she wants to find Charles.
>
> **Student:** Right here in this picture, Charles is in his mom's shadow, it's over him. That's how his mom is again. Charles is overpowered.
>
> **Teacher:** Overshadowing, overpowering. She's always there, isn't she?
>
> **Student:** And the hat. The hat always represents the mom always being there.
>
> **Teacher:** Shadows and hats, they're overpowering. They're always there. She's always in control. No matter what Charles wants to do.
>
> **Student:** On that one page with the teeter-totter, she's like up higher because he's weak and she's overpowering. Like she has more power than he did, so she's higher than him.
>
> **Teacher:** OK, and you might want to look at it that she not afraid to be up high. She climbs higher in the trees. She's done all that. She's explored it. He's been so conservative and reserved. She's not afraid. Good.

Display, Procedural, Process, and Inquiry Questions

The Challenge: Many of the questions teachers ask are literal recall questions. These recall questions privilege the text over the readers' interpretations and focus students' attention on what has been written by the author rather than what has been thought by the reader. Trying to break teachers of this habit is difficult because asking literal recall questions has a long history in school. However, breaking this interaction pattern is essential for moving from naming or recalling elements of text and illustrations to interpreting and comprehending what has been read.

Our Intentions: By demonstrating a wider range of questioning techniques, we hope to provide teachers ways to ask questions that move beyond the literal text and support readers' interpretive strategies.

Lesson Overview: The lesson provided below will focus on using inquiry questions to support interpretation in literature discussions. The differences between inquiry and literal recall questions will be described before explaining how this lesson would proceed.

There are four types of questions that are primarily used during literature discussions and other classroom interactions (see Figure 3.4).

Display or rote questions focus exclusively on what is in the text and images themselves. Process questions focus on how students come to understandings or their interpretive techniques. Procedural questions focus on the expectations and procedures that support discussions. Inquiry questions provide for a range of acceptable answers rather than one main idea or authorized interpretation, open up discussions to consider multiple interpretations and possibilities, view the text as a point of departure rather than the object of study, and go beyond literal recall to utilize "higher-order" thought processes.

FIG. 3.4 *Types of Questions*

1. Display/Rote
2. Process/Reasoning
3. Procedural/Expectations
4. Inquiry/Exploratory

Language of Instruction:

Good morning, Readers! Today we are going to talk about asking questi[on]
kinds of questions teachers ask. To start, let's talk about your experiences wit[h]
in school. What kinds of questions have teachers asked you in the past? [
Let's take a look at the list of questions I have displayed on the board behin[d]
Figure 3.5). We have been talking about noticings, generating interpretations, and co-
elaboration for some time now, but here I have listed some questions that go along with
each of these interpretive strategies. As we read today's picturebook, *Rose Blanche* by
Roberto Innocenti (1985), I would like you to pay attention to the text and illustrations
and the ideas in this book that relate to our discussions about the Holocaust and Internment. When we are finished, we are going to try some of the questions from our
chart to see if these support better discussions than the ones we talked about earlier. We
want to change the types of questions we pose, change who asks the questions, and
change how these questions affect our discussions.

Instructional Trajectory:

The goal of asking more sophisticated, open-ended questions is to develop more sophisticated interpretations. Better questioning techniques should have an influence on
what students attend to and the types of interpretations they construct. We want to ask
honest questions, questions we don't know the answers to, if we expect to receive honest answers from students in reply.

Classroom Artifacts:

The following list in Figure 3.5 should be used as an example of the types of questions
we ask, not simply a list of questions to be asked each time a book is finished. As teachers, we need to shift from asking primarily literal questions to asking questions that
open possibilities and spaces for discussion.

FIG. 3.5 *Inquiry Question Examples*

Focus on Noticing:

What are your initial impressions?

What caught your attention?

What seemed unique, peculiar?

Focus on Generating Interpretations:

What might these noticings mean?

How does this connect with what you know?

What other meanings are possible?

Focus on Co-Elaboration:

Have you considered others' ideas?

How do alternative interpretations affect your ideas?

What do these ideas mean for your future reading?

Closing Comments: The types of questions that teachers ask have a direct relationship to the types of answers students provide. Unless we begin asking better questions, we probably shouldn't expect better discussions. One challenge to this theory is that simply asking better questions may not be sufficient to change the types of discussions we have. As long as students believe that the correct answers are found hidden in the text or in the teacher's head, then those will be the only places they look for them. The more transparent, rigorous, and clear the expectations we set for our discussions (see Lesson 3.1 for more information), the better chance we have of having more sophisticated discussions.

He Said, She Said, I Think

The Challenge: Getting students to listen to one another, not just the teacher, during literature discussions takes a lot of practice. Students have been programmed to respond directly to the teacher, bypassing the comments, ideas, and interpretations of other students. In order to get students to respond to peers, they need to begin listening to one another and offer their comments directly to one another rather than through the teacher.

Our Intentions: This lesson is designed to get students to listen to everyone, and use what is offered as the foundation for their subsequent comments. The focus is on summarizing what has been said, stating another student's position, and then adding one's own ideas to the conversation. This lesson supports the consideration of students' interpretations and the negotiation of meanings in a community of readers.

Lesson Overview: Students are taught how to begin their comments with the statement, "he said this, and she said that, and I was thinking. . . ." Obviously, the pronouns may vary but the overall intention is to get students to take up from what has been offered and add to the literary discussion in meaningful ways.

Language of Instruction: Good morning, Readers! Today we are going to play around with the language of our responses. Let me explain what I mean. I have been noticing that when we finish reading a text and are talking about it, many of you don't seem to be paying attention to one another and always look at me when you are offering ideas. Now, of course it's perfectly all right that you look at me when you are offering ideas, but what if you are making a comment about someone else's ideas? Shouldn't you look at them as well? So here is what we are going to try. Before you offer your own comments, I want you to refer to what others have been saying. Let me give you an example. Yesterday, we talked about the picturebook *Martin's Big Words* by Doreen Rappaport (2001). During our discussion, Morgan suggested that Martin Luther King Jr. was a hero, but not like war heroes because he didn't believe in violence. After that, Vaughn said that people don't have to go to war to become heroes. Since I had been listening closely to both of you, I could have said, "Well, Morgan thinks that Martin Luther King Jr. was a hero, and Vaughn thinks that people don't have to go to war to become heroes, and I was thinking that heroes are simply people who do really good things for other people, often risking their own lives, and it doesn't matter where they do it." Can you see what I have done here? I began by referring to what one student said, then another student, and then I added my own ideas. In order to be able to do this, I had to pay close attention to what everyone was saying. That is an important part of this lesson. I really want everyone to listen to everyone's ideas, and I want everyone to add to our conversation.

So, here's what we will do today. After we finish reading today's picturebook, *Amelia and Eleanor Go for a Ride* by Pam Muñoz Ryan (1999), we will start off by talking as usual, and then I will ask you to try the He Said, She Said, I Think strategy. Let's give it a try and see if this helps our discussions.

Instructional Trajectory: The real focus of this lesson is to get students to listen to one another and not just talk directly to the teacher all the time. If this lesson begins to work in our literature discussions, we may begin to see evidence of its effectiveness in discussions in other areas of the curriculum.

Classroom Artifacts: We could chart the various He Said, She Said, I Think comments, but this is primarily a discussion strategy.

Closing Comments: Although this discussion strategy may seem a bit inauthentic and possibly overly structured, the goal of having students listen to one another and consider what is being offered is an important objective. In an effective community of readers, children listen to one another and consider each other's interpretations and contributions. Students have to learn to summarize what has been offered, paraphrase what has been said, and offer ideas that are new to the conversation. These are all important skills to develop.

Critical Junctures

The Challenge: There are times when students offer interesting ideas and teachers don't recognize the possibilities in what has been said. Frank has been referring to these moments in a discussion as *critical junctures*. These are places in a literature discussion where the teacher has more than one way to proceed and must make a decision about whether to follow the direction of a students' interpretation or redirect the conversation. Sensitive listening, an extensive knowledge of literature, and the ability to effectively facilitate discussions are all important qualities for teachers to develop.

Our Intentions: This lesson will be a bit different from the others in this section in that there is no section focusing on the Language of Instruction. Instead, we offer a transcript from an intermediate grade literature discussion that highlights the concept of critical junctures. Our goal is to get teachers to recognize these situations in their own discussions and make more effective choices for how to continue. A prominent characteristic of critical junctures is that students offer interpretations that go beyond the literal level of the text. We need to realize when this happens, and acknowledge that the most important contributions go beyond naming literal elements in the text and illustrations and instead involve interpretations and inferring more sophisticated meanings.

Lesson Overview: The discussion we feature in Figure 3.6 focused on the book *The Three Pigs* by David Wiesner (2001) in an intermediate grade classroom. The class was discussing the pages of the picturebook where the pigs are illustrated in different styles and one pig is changing color and detail as he comes out of one section of the illustration. The discussion picks up from that point.

During this discussion, the students offered several opportunities for the teacher to expand on, to go deeper with the students, and at these moments, the teacher seemed to simply move on to get more comments from students. For example, when a student said that Wiesner used different colors to make it look like a different author or illustrator did the book, the teacher might have taken this comment a bit further to explore what the student was referring to.

Instructional Trajectory: There is an inherent tension between a teacher's need to pace a lesson and her duty to remain open to tangents that may yield fantastic student insights. There are times when wandering is counterproductive; however, there are times when we have to wander in our thoughts to construct meaning. Pacing is important for lessons to move forward given the limited amount of time we have in the school day. But, sometimes we have to

FIG. 3.6
The Three Pigs *Transcript*

Student 1: And when they go to the dragon, too. Because the pictures are in black and white in the dragon part and when they start getting out of the illustration they turn color again.

Student 2: Oh yeah, like when they go "hey diddle diddle."

Teacher: And then, what did you say? You said that the dragon pages are black and white but then …

Student 1: They're getting out, they turn color again.

Teacher: Who is *they*?

Student 1: The pigs.

Teacher: So, why do you think that is? Because they're colored here?

Student 3: Because, they're not in it all the way.

Teacher: Who's not in it all the way and what is it?

Student 3: The pigs are not in the page all the way.

Student 1: Because I think they're going to a different book and like the author is pretending a different author made that book and so maybe he wanted to make it black and white so that the pigs would go in a different story and turn the same color. That is what the book is supposed to be.

Teacher: OK, did you hear that? Did you hear what she said? OK, because it is interesting. Because the pigs out here, they're colored. But the little pigs in there are not. Does anyone have a different thought as to why they are and why they're not colored and why on this page these two guys are not? What do you think?

Student 4: Because he's coming out of that page and that story is black and white.

Teacher: Good! What did you notice besides color? Is there anything besides the color? Is there anything else you noticed about the illustrations?

Student 3: Over here on the second page. There's those two pigs. How did the pig carry all those bricks? I am wondering how can the pig carry all those bricks when it's just the one pig and bricks are like heavy?

Teacher: The bricks are really heavy, OK.

Student 3: And, on page 2 the pig [*Turn pages in the book*] the village one had the straw on his back who put the straws on his back?

Teacher: OK, so who put the straw on his back?

wander to wonder. We believe that both are important and that every lesson tries to balance the need to move forward and reach completion with the need to deeply consider what is at hand.

Classroom Artifacts: Because this is a discussion strategy, there is no chart or artifact other than better discussions.

Closing Comments: The point of this lesson and the reason we shared this transcript is to get teachers to pay attention to what they endorse with their comments, and what they miss when they don't try to go beyond the literal level of the text. The fact that the one pig had a hard time carrying bricks is certainly less important than the fact that one student understood and discussed a central feature of this story: that the pigs went in and out of stories and Wiesner demonstrated this through the use of illustrative techniques and color. As teachers, we need to develop our own interpretive repertoires if we expect to help students develop theirs.

Dialogue Blockers

The Challenge: As much as we try to encourage students to pay close attention and listen to one another, there are certain characteristics of discussions and participants that block this shift from recitation into dialogue. These characteristics have been studied by researchers like Debra Myhill (Myhill, Jones, and Hooper 2006) and Robin Alexander (2006) in the United Kingdom, and Courtney Cazden (2001) and Martin Nystrand (1997) in the United States. Making the characteristics of effective dialogue and the phenomenon that impede this type of discussion known to students is an important starting point for decreasing their negative effects on literature discussions.

Our Intentions: The goal of this lesson is not to criticize students for their discussion styles, rather it is to make clear those things we do that prevent the class from having more effective discussions.

Lesson Overview: This lesson is intended to generate a list of Dialogue Blockers for students to consider. The list will begin with what students offer and their perspectives, and will include some ideas offered by the teacher (see Figure 3.7 for my additions to the list).

Language of Instruction: Good morning, Readers! I have been paying close attention to our literature discussions recently and have a few comments to make. Sometimes we really seem to listen to one another, allow each other to offer ideas, and are respectful of one another's interpretations. And then there are some times where we don't do as well. Have any of you recognized this, too?

I was hoping that maybe you had noticed this. I think we should talk today about those things that prevent us from having those "grand conversations" that we want to have. Let's start by having you share some things that you think prevent us from having better discussions and I will write them on a chart for us to refer to during our discussions. [*Group offers ideas.*]

Instructional Trajectory: The lesson should extend to all discussions thereafter. However, without referring to the chart from time to time, many of these suggestions are forgotten. We suggest posting this chart near the discussion area so that students can refer to it whenever challenges arise. Having students involved in the creation of the chart adds to their investment and increases the possibility of these characteristics taking hold for longer periods.

Classroom Artifacts: One chart will be generated by the class. This often includes simple directives like: pay attention, be nice, listen, and look at the speaker. In addition to these ideas, we offer for teachers a second chart (see Figure 3.7) that they may wish to use to include some ideas on their classroom chart.

Closing Comments: It is not simply one's ability to analyze literature and offer ideas that creates opportunities for quality literature discussions. Each member must be respectful of one another's thoughts, learn ways to enter a conversation, support other's participation in the discussions, and learn how to disagree without attacking one another. Changing the way that students talk about books takes time. Being patient and supportive and sharing what you notice with students helps make change permanent.

FIG. 3.7
Dialogue Blockers

1. Dominating Voices—We can't talk all the time.

2. Passive Participants—Everyone has to participate in our discussions.

3. Lack of Time—We won't start discussions when we feel rushed.

4. Focus on Debating (Winning the Discussion)—Discussions are about learning, not winning.

5. Seeking Consensus, Not Possibilities—Everyone does not have to agree, we just have to consider what others have offered.

6. Defensive Attitudes—Stand firm with your ideas, but not so firm you don't consider other possibilities.

Reading Across Genres

Genres are types of texts that contain similar features and function. In elementary and middle school classrooms, the reading and writing curricula are often constructed around prominent genres, including research reports, personal narrative, poetry, historical fiction, and realistic fiction. While it is certainly important to help readers understand these genres to be successful in school, there are many genres that exist outside school that are just as important for students to read and analyze, including advertisements, websites, billboards, and magazines. We need to connect the genres that are read at home and in school to expand our definition of what it means to be a proficient reader and honor those texts that are important to children and their particular cultures. Organizing reading lessons by genres provides opportunities for students to make connections across texts, compare various books within the same genre, and understand how the various features of a particular genre work.

The lessons included in this strand are intended to enhance readers' understandings of a variety of genres as they analyze the textual and visual features of a given genre, and consider the role of genres in the larger context of society. As readers become familiar with the similarities and differences among various genres they will be able to adjust their reading practices and use the textual and visual features of a genre as a resource for comprehension.

The comprehension lessons in this section include:

4.1 My Genres Box

4.2 Analyzing Genres

4.3 Analyzing Realistic Fiction

4.4 Reading Multigenre Picturebooks

4.5 Approaching Historical Fiction

4.6 Analyzing Advertisements

4.7 Reading Magazines

4.8 Reading Biographies

My Genres Box

The Challenge: In school, readers are required to become familiar with specific genres contained in the district's standards documents, curriculum framework, or which feature prominently on their standardized tests. Unfortunately, this means the reading students do in their daily lives is often not endorsed, recognized, or taught in schools. As classroom teachers we need to expand what we mean by "being literate" and acknowledge and endorse those genres and types of texts that are important to students in their lives outside of schools.

Our Intentions: This lesson gives readers a chance to highlight the genres that are relevant to them, and to share how these selections provide insights into their literate identities. Creating a Genres That Tell About Me Box gives children an authentic opportunity for reading a variety of genres that interest them or to tell about those literate activities that are relevant to their lives. We want readers to be acknowledged for the wide variety of materials they read and to help children make selections of new genres.

Lesson Overview: Students will collect and place into a Genres That Tell About Me Box (or Genres Box) examples of genres and specific texts that are important to them or represent important aspects of their lives. Students will also brainstorm lists of genres they intend to read in the future.

Language of Instruction: Good morning, Readers! Today we are going to think about literature and how our choices of what we read tells something about our identities. Rather than write an autobiography about our reading lives, we are going to put together a collection of texts and genres that tells something about who we are. You may consider favorite and not-so-favorite selections, genres you plan on reading, those that have been read to you, or those that you feel you should have read but never did. With each selection you will need to include some explanations about why you enjoy these particular genres and why you stay away from others. Eventually, our Genre Boxes will lead to a writing project, but today we will just focus on collecting a variety of genres and explaining why they are important to us. The reason to do this is that what we read tells us a lot about ourselves, and provides an opportunity to celebrate all the kinds of reading we do on a daily basis. Many of us think that just because we are not reading novels we are not readers. Nothing could be farther from the truth! This lesson is about sharing and celebrating all the types of reading we do and demonstrating how literate we all are.

I have asked one student, Chandler, to model alongside me how we might brainstorm a list of texts and genres (see Figure 4.1). We worked on this list together because I think

Suzette (teacher)	Chandler (student)
Journal articles	Poetry
Children's literature	Humorous books
Children's published writing	*Ranger Rick*
Parenting books	All genres of picturebooks
Travel brochures	Directions to electronic journal
Home and garden magazines	Tamagotchi instructions
Numerous cookbooks	Junior cookbook
Cooking magazines	Basal anthology
Murder mysteries	Realistic fiction novels
School newsletters	Scary stories
Emails	Notes from sister
Websites	Letters
Parenting ideas	Thank-you notes
Craft ideas	Birthday invitations
Research for teaching	Email
TV Guide	Reading journal
Science Fair books	Personal readers
Books on education	Text books
Remodeling books and magazines	Informational text
Toy manuals	Reread own journal
Furniture assembly instructions	Journal stories
CNN news footers	*TV Guide*
Students' reading logs (any log)	Directions for preparing food
Letters	Grocery list
Thank-you notes	Weekly letters from teachers
Notes from daughters	Notes from teacher in reading log
Personal journal	Notes from classmates
I Chat	Images
Resumes	*American Girl* magazines
Camera and video camera manuals	Songs
Bedtime stories	Comics
Newspaper	Menus
Menus	Newspaper

FIG. 4.1 *Possible Genres*

it is important for you to see how I would brainstorm a list, but I also want you to see how someone in your class might do this as well. So we thought about our lists ahead of time and now we are going to share the genres we have selected and how they might reveal things about ourselves.

As you can see, the list might really keep going on forever. What we need to do now is to select those genres that are really important to us. Chandler and I will each select two genres from our list and explain why our selection is important and what it might reveal about us.

Teacher: I think one of the most important selections on my list might be a cookbook, both printed and online versions. I am not the most creative cook, so in order for my family not to eat the same thing every night I refer to cookbooks all the time. It is really important that my family eat healthy meals so I select a lot of recipes from healthy food web sites and *Cooking Light* magazine. As you can see, I read three different genres on the same topic: websites, cookbooks, and magazines.

My second most important genre is letters. I love getting letters from my daughters. They are always writing to let me know what party I am invited to, when not to enter their rooms, stuff they would like, to tell me they are sorry, and to tell me they love me. I write letters back to them as well. Those two genres or reading selections tell a lot about me. I will collect as many of these items as I can to put in my Genres Box.

Chandler: I really like to read cookbooks. I like to cook and I want to cook sometimes. I like cooking because it is fun and you get to use all different types of food. I hope one day to have the first kid cooking show on the Food Network. I love to try out different recipes and wear an apron. This is the first time I have ever owned a cookbook so I haven't really read in this genre before.

The second genre is my Tamagotchi instruction book because I like to play with my Tamagotchi. I use the book to know about the buttons and when to press them to feed or play with my Tamagotchi. It was confusing at first but it makes sense after you have played with it for a while. I read parts, but not all of my other instruction books to know how to play with some toys I have, especially my talking dog. I couldn't get him to talk so I needed to read the instructions.

OK class, we are each going to sit and think about those genres and texts that we read in and out of school, and especially those that are relevant to our lives and important for showing our literate lives.

Instructional Trajectory:	Students will become more aware of themselves as readers and hopefully be able to articulate their reading habits during informal and formal conversations with classmates, as well as the teacher. This lesson also helps build a community of readers as students begin to see the similarities and differences in their reading identities. Children who read genres that are not directly endorsed in school settings will also begin to see themselves as readers.
Classroom Artifacts:	Class charts containing brainstorm lists to demonstrate the kinds of reading, texts, and genres students might include will be created.
Closing Comments:	Creating a Genres That Tell About Me Box requires children to attend to what they read. First and foremost, we want them to see themselves as readers regardless of their reading choices because that can have a lasting impact on their attitudes toward reading. This lesson will also highlight what students read and what they don't read, and this will allow the teacher to guide them into reading a wider variety of texts and genres.

Analyzing Genres

The Challenge: Students read and use a variety of genres on a daily basis. They need to understand that genres are not static characteristics of texts but change according to the needs and uses of texts in a particular society. Looking at the forms various genres can take will help students to consider their purposes in the real world.

Our Intentions: This lesson will require students to attend to the various forms of genres and how form can be a resource for constructing meaning. Looking at a variety of genres will help readers to understand that genres and their forms may change frequently based on the reasons for using them.

Lesson Overview: In this lesson, students will be exposed to a variety of genres to consider their forms and functions, and how these are used to communicate meaning. Students will analyze a variety of resources and the forms they include.

Language of Instruction: Good morning, Readers! Today we are going to consider a variety of genres. I have gathered together some brochures, letters, stories, webpages, magazines, advertisements, newspapers, poems, textbooks, spelling lists, video-game instruction booklets, comic books, CD cases, and some other genres. For today's lesson, we are going to focus on what they look like and how their form can tell us a lot about each genre. Just as we have learned how to approach picturebooks (see Lesson 2.1), I would like us to look at how we approach these various genres and attend to the forms they utilize.

I have hung many of these on the chalkboard or placed them on the table for you to peruse, and I would like you to name the genres based only on how they look to you. As you name them, be prepared to discuss how you knew it was that particular genre and I will write your ideas on the chart next to it (see Figure 4.2). Then we will look at each genre and read them a little more in depth to fill out the rest of our chart.

Now let's take a closer look at one particular genre and how it comes in many different forms. Here are five different kinds of brochures. Even though we might be able to identify them all as brochures, there are a lot of differences within this genre. The differences exist because of the purposes for using the brochure, the content of the brochure, and the intended audience. I have brochures from the Grand Canyon, Six Flags Amusement Park, an orthodontist, an interior designer, and from our local baseball team. I am going to put you into small groups and give each group a set of brochures. I would like you read through the brochures and answer the questions or prompts in Figure 4.3.

FIG. 4.2
Genre Examples Chart

Genre	Description	Why is the form important?	Language or Images
Brochure	❖ Folded 3 times ❖ Has images and text ❖ Is very colorful	❖ Can be viewed easily ❖ Catches the eye ❖ Can fit a lot of information if you fold it ❖ Can be read and more quickly understood	❖ Images are photographs ❖ Words are persuasive ❖ Heading and text are smaller than pictures
Spelling list	❖ Numbered 1–15 ❖ Alphabetical order ❖ One word per line	❖ To help you study and see the words ❖ To call out more easily when doing a pretest	❖ No images ❖ Single words only
Poem	❖ 10 lines ❖ Some lines consist of only one word ❖ Has line breaks	❖ Form is more emotionally expressive ❖ Line breaks tell you how to read it	❖ No image (this one) ❖ Words rhyme ❖ A rhythm created
Webpage	❖ Is on the computer ❖ Has a title ❖ Has links to other parts of the webpage	❖ Links would not work if it were paper ❖ Title lets you know what it is about	❖ Words and images ❖ Advertisements in boxes ❖ Many different colors ❖ Different colored text ❖ Links change colors ❖ Colored links change when hit

When you have finished we'll discuss the various forms of these brochures as a whole class. Pay close attention to the way particular forms are used and the possible purposes for these forms.

FIG. 4.3 *Questions for Analyzing Brochures*

1. Describe the form. How do the forms differ? How are they similar?

2. Describe the language and images used. What is the interplay between image and text?

3. What is the purpose for the brochure? How does the form fit or not fit with their purpose?

Instructional Trajectory: Understanding genre in general will affect all that readers do. Attending to the form will add to their repertoire of reading strategies. Being able to read within one particular genre and analyze the forms and their accompanying functions will help readers read across genres as well.

Classroom Artifacts: Classroom charts could be constructed to organize and record thoughts on the various genres and their forms.

Closing Comments: Genres are a social entity and are constructed based on their purposes, audiences, and functions within any given society. As students become more familiar with the functional aspects of a particular genre they will be better equipped to take a critical stance toward the various genres they encounter.

Analyzing Realistic Fiction

The Challenge: Realistic fiction is widely read in most elementary and middle school classrooms. There are numerous titles available and students relate to these stories written about events children their age experience. However, we should not assume children understand how to comprehend this genre just because it is frequently read to them. This lesson provides opportunities to help children become critical readers of realistic fiction by creating criteria for judging it.

Our Intentions: It is important for readers to become critical evaluators of realistic fiction. We certainly could provide criteria from any children's literature textbook about what makes a quality example of realistic fiction; however, we believe it is much more powerful and engaging for students to attend to the features of the genre, and create criteria for themselves.

Lesson Overview: Students will begin investigating this genre by looking at the realistic fiction titles they have read themselves, and those read aloud in class. Students will then create a list of criteria for selecting and evaluating realistic fiction based on their selections.

Language of Instruction: Good morning, Readers! Today I have asked you all to bring your favorite and most interesting realistic fiction books with you to our group. As you recall, we defined realistic fiction as those stories that tell about situations occurring in the real world during current times. The events in realistic fiction may not have actually happened, but they might have happened. Let's begin by thinking about why you selected the books you did. How did you know your selections were examples of realistic fiction? Let's create a chart listing the characteristics of realistic fiction (see Figure 4.4). Tell me why you think your book is an example of realistic fiction.

FIG. 4.4 *Characteristics for Realistic Fiction*

> ❖ The main character was our age.
>
> ❖ The setting was believable or actual places.
>
> ❖ I went through what the character went through.
>
> ❖ It reminded me of something that happened to me.
>
> ❖ I have a sister just like the one in the book.
>
> ❖ There wasn't any magic in the book.

FIG. 4.5 *Additional Characteristics for Realistic Fiction*

❖ There wasn't an author's note saying this was a true story.

❖ The book was in the fiction section of the library.

❖ It does not say biography or autobiography on it.

❖ We know that the story could be true but it was not.

❖ If it is good, when you read the book, you do not know that it is not real.

It seems that we have discussed the "realistic" part of realistic fiction, but what makes these stories fictional? Why are your books realistic *fiction*? Let's add to our chart some ideas about the fictional part (see Figure 4.5).

These are great lists. Let's talk about one of your selections. I see someone chose *Smoky Night* by Eve Bunting (1994). We know the book was about the Los Angeles riots that occurred in 1992. Eve Bunting wrote a story about something that actually occurred. The story is about real events in history, but the characters are fictional. Is this an example of realistic fiction or historical fiction or another genre? Turn to a partner and discuss your ideas on this book. [*Discuss the differences between historical and realistic fiction.*]

Now, let's chart out what you like the most about these examples of realistic fiction. What about the books that we have read so far this year? Are they examples of quality realistic fiction? Let's chart out all of these ideas and see if we can create our own criteria for evaluating realistic fiction (see Figure 4.6).

We might want to ask ourselves some additional questions when we are evaluating realistic fiction. We can ask ourselves: Did anyone find misunderstandings in books? Were there books or parts of books that you felt where the author didn't quite understand

FIG. 4.6 *Criteria for Evaluating Realistic Fiction*

❖ Addresses important social issues.

❖ The characters are believable.

❖ The characters talked like real children.

❖ I understood the events in the story.

❖ I could relate to the main character.

❖ I could not wait to read to find out what happened next in the story.

❖ I learned about something new about myself or the world.

❖ The ending was good, not always happy, but good.

❖ I could imagine the story happening.

what it was like to be a boy, or a girl, or a different race? How are girls and boys portrayed in these books? What messages are being sent about different social issues? Is more than one side presented? Let's use these criteria and questions to evaluate the selections each of you brought to the group today.

Instructional Trajectory: Discussing criteria and characteristics of particular genres should take place with every genre to which we expose students. An analysis of each genre should affect students' writing in that genre as well.

Classroom Artifacts: Charts of genre characteristics and criteria for selecting quality realistic fiction should be constructed.

Closing Comments: Creating the characteristics and evaluation criteria empowers children as they begin to think about those titles they know and learn to evaluate. It may also affect their selection process. This lesson also gives readers tools to analyze and evaluate those books that might not appeal to them. It is also a great chance for the teacher to provide students with new titles and expand the criteria for selecting and comprehending realistic fiction.

Reading Multigenre Picturebooks

The Challenge: Many picturebooks on the market today include multiple genres, meaning there may be examples of more than one genre in a single picturebook. It is important to help students think about how the multiple genres within a text influence their reading.

Our Intentions: During this lesson, we call attention to the multiple genres within a single picturebook and how these genres work together to create a whole story. Students will analyze the individual genres as well as the text as a whole. Students will then reflect on the choices the authors made and how effective the authors were in combining various genres.

Lesson Overview: We will read aloud and discuss a wonderful picturebook that contain multiple genres: *The Jolly Postman or Other People's Letters* by Janet and Allan Ahlburg (1986). We will begin by reading and discussing this picturebook and completing a Noticings, Connections, Wonderings chart (see Lesson 2.1). Then students will be asked to identify the various genres found throughout the book, analyze why these genres have been selected, how they added to the book as a whole, and then consider the book as a whole again.

Language of Instruction: Good morning, Readers! Today we are going to read *The Jolly Postman or Other People's Letters*. Stop me as I am reading if you have some comments, want to point out something, or are wondering about a particular part. When we are finished we will complete a Noticings, Connections, Wonderings (NCW) chart, so I would like you to be thinking of what you might want to share about the book. [*Read and discuss book and add to the NCW chart.*]

Now, I am going to read the book again, and I would like you to think about the different genres that are used in the book. [*Read book again.*] Can anyone name any of the genres that were found in this picturebook? [*Discuss.*] I would like you to think about each genre and what you know about that genre in the world. In other words, how and where are these genres used in our everyday lives? For example, many of us receive flyers in the mail. They provide information, come from a particular company, and we either get excited about the contents or throw them out in the trash. The flyer about the witch, however, is funny! It's funny because it is a real-life genre sent to a fictional fairy-tale character. Taking a genre from one context and placing it in another can be very creative and often humorous. In order to appreciate the humor you need to know the use of the genre in other contexts.

So, let's consider how the various genres in this picturebook affect the book as a whole. I have a guide sheet to help us with our discussion (see Figure 4.7).

FIG. 4.7 *Reading Multigenre Picturebooks*

1. Name the genres in the book.

2. How are the genres used in the real world, and how are they used in this book?

3. What does each genre add to the whole book?

4. How does the author tie all the genres together?

5. Were there any genres you think could have added to the book that were missing?

Instructional Trajectory: Students will begin to attend to the nature of genres in various multigenre picture-books. By analyzing the genres in the real world, readers will begin to understand and analyze why particular authors chose to write in this manner. Students might begin to attend to various genres in their classroom discussions as well as in their responses to literature. This will also give them some support when deciding on genres for their own writing.

Classroom Artifacts: Classroom charts and small-group guide sheets can be created.

Closing Comments: This lesson helps children understand the nature of multiple genre books and gives them some strategies for approaching, analyzing, and evaluating the various genres in these picturebooks.

Approaching Historical Fiction

The Challenge: Historical fiction is a prominent genre in most intermediate grade classrooms. Students may develop misconceptions about historical fiction, thinking that stories in this genre are true, or conversely, that everything is imaginary. We need to help readers discern and separate the fictional from the historically accurate as they begin to explore and learn about historical fiction.

Our Intentions: This lesson will focus on helping students read and determine the fictional and historically accurate elements in historical fiction, and give them strategies for dealing with both aspects of this genre.

Lesson Overview: After reading aloud a historical fiction picturebook, students will be guided through a lesson that helps them to analyze various literary and visual elements of the text to determine what is fictional and what is historically accurate.

Language of Instruction: Good morning, Readers! Today, we are going to read the picturebook *The Bracelet* by Yoshiko Uchida (1993), illustrated by Joanna Yardley, once again. This book fits into our study of the impact of World War II on American citizens and will also fit into our study of historical fiction. To begin, we are going to focus on some strategies for reading historical fiction. Today, as I am reading this picturebook, I would like you to think about the genre of historical fiction. If you remember, in historical fiction some aspects of the story have been made up and some aspects of the story are based on actual historical events. In every example of historical fiction, how much of the story is fictional can really vary. For example, in The Magic Treehouse series by Mary Pope Osborne, the characters go traveling back in time, which would make this like some of the books in the fantasy genre. However, where the characters went were actual historical periods, which would fit into the historical fiction genre.

In *The Bracelet*, it is not so obvious what aspects of the story are fictional and what are historically accurate, primarily because the story is based on the author's personal experiences. Let's review what we know about Yoshiko Uchida. She is a Japanese American and was born in California in 1922. During World War II, the Japanese bombed Pearl Harbor and at that time Yoshiko was going to college at the University of California, Berkley. She was ordered by the United States government to leave college and was placed in an internment camp. She has written many books for young readers describing this time in her history as she dealt with hatred, racism, and discrimination.

The Bracelet	Historically Accurate	Fictionalized	How do we know?
Setting			
Characters			
Plot			
Illustrations			

FIG. 4.8
Analyzing Elements of
The Bracelet

I would like for us to think about the literary and visual elements in *The Bracelet* and how the characters and historical events are portrayed in this picturebook. I think that it is really important for us to be able to identify what is fictionalized and what is based on historical research or personal experience. Let's create a chart (see Figure 4.8) of the various story elements and provide some evidence for considering whether these elements are fictional or historically accurate.

Let's consider the categories in this chart and how we might fill it in. After we complete this chart together it can serve as a model for your own historical fiction picturebook analysis.

Instructional Trajectory: This lesson will help readers ascertain the fictional and historical aspects of any historical fiction selection they choose to read. We might expect to see this continue in our future discussions and responses to literature. Like many of the lessons in this strand, the goal is to provide readers with guides or criteria for analyzing and comprehending a variety of genres.

Classroom Artifacts: A whole class T-chart for analyzing historical fiction, and small-group T-charts will be the primary artifacts for this lesson (see Figure 4.8).

Closing Comments: Historical fiction is a great resource for expanding historical understandings. It maintains a balance between the fictional aspects and accurate historical events. Readers should have strategies to be able to read, comprehend, and evaluate various historical fiction novels and picturebooks. This lesson helps them separate the two aspects of historical fiction.

Analyzing Advertisements

The Challenge: Children are inundated with advertisements on a daily basis. We spend a great deal of time helping students read and understand fantasy, fairy tales, realistic fiction, and historical fiction, yet we may fall short helping them critically read the types of genres they experience in their daily lives. In order to read advertisements, students need to become familiar with visual design and the concept of an "intended audience" so they may understand how advertisements position readers to feel and act in certain ways. If we teach students to think critically about advertisements, they will be more aware of the impact various design choices, images, and texts have on them as consumers.

Our Intentions: Students who think about audience in advertisements are attending to the language, structure, and overall choice of genre and how that affects their reading of any given text. It is the goal of this lesson to help readers think critically about the choices an author or artist makes when creating an advertisement.

Lesson Overview: Students will analyze advertisements found in a variety of sources. They will consider how the advertisement changes depending on context, and how the language and images are geared to a particular audience.

Language of Instruction: Good morning, Readers! Today we are going to investigate a number of advertisements. As we do so, we are going to consider two things. First, I would like us to consider how advertisers make choices concerning language and images to appeal to a certain audiences. Second, we need to consider how the advertisements change depending on their contexts. In other words, when these advertisements appear in different magazines, on the radio, television, Internet, or posted on billboards they change in many ways.

On the floor in front of you I have placed a variety of advertisements for you to consider. On the screen I have projected one I found on the Internet. We have a few magazine advertisements, one from a fashion magazine, one from a sports magazine, and one from a home-decorating magazine. We also have ads from newspapers, pictures of billboards from around town, T-shirts, and I have a DVD of some television commercials.

The first thing I would like us to do is to think about the intended audience for each of these advertisements. Let me give you an example of what I am thinking about. [*I put on the board an advertisement for* SpongeBob SquarePants *toys that are linked to Burger King found in* Teen Magazine.] How can we tell who the intended audience might be? Is there more than one intended audience? First, I notice the advertisement highlights the toys and not the food. The ad is geared toward younger readers who might like to get the kid's meal at this fast-food restaurant. It is a two-page spread with nothing but pictures of a giant SpongeBob and the second page is filled with images and names of the ten new toys at Burger King. Notice how they use the word *collect*. I think about how that might influence a young reader. It might sound neat to have all of them, or to show your friends that you have all of them. At the very bottom there is a white bar that is showing the healthier choices you can make at Burger King. So, the ad might also be geared toward parents who are willing to take their child to the restaurant, as children cannot get there on their own.

What if this ad were on the radio? You would need to hear SpongeBob's voice describing the toys and how you can collect all of them. I wonder how the healthy choices would be dealt with on the radio, as it is such a small portion of the printed advertisement. Each context changes the appearance of the advertisement and what might be included. We need to always consider the context when we are thinking about the intended audience.

I would like you to work with a partner and look at the rest of the advertisements in front of you and see if you can identify the audience for each advertisement. Once you do, support your ideas with examples from the advertisement as you refer to the language, fonts, and the kinds of visual images included. Then consider what would happen to the advertisement if it were in a different context. When you are done we will share what we found out about intended audiences and how it affects our reading.

Instructional Trajectory: Helping children see the connection between advertisements also helps them see how they are influenced by various elements, which have been manipulated to match the interest of a particular audience. The context for an advertisement, as for any text, has an impact on how readers approach it and how they interpret it.

Classroom Artifacts: Students can create guide sheets to organize and record their ideas on audience as they interact with the advertisements and primary source documents. We usually list some questions that we want students to ask themselves as they approach an advertisement (see Figure 4.9).

FIG. 4.9 *Questions for Analyzing Advertisements*

What is made salient?

What is in focus, out of focus?

Where are components located in the advertisement (top/bottom)?

Who is portrayed, not portrayed?

How are text and images connected?

Who is the intended audience?

What is the "catch" or "hook"?

Closing Comments: Analyzing an advertisement is an important reading practice for students. Advertisers of children's toys, games, fast foods, and soft drinks create advertisements to appeal to young children's needs, interests, identities, and fears. Most young readers are not able to understand how particular advertisements make them feel and act. As readers engage in this lesson students become aware of how images, written text, and design choices are configured for a particular audience and how readers are being asked to engage with various texts.

Reading Magazines

The Challenge: There are many young readers who wait with great anticipation to receive their *Ranger Rick* or other magazines in the mail. Magazines are an important part of many readers' reading life. In fact, we know of very few people who don't subscribe to at least one magazine. We need to provide children with some tools for exploring and comprehending magazines to enhance their reading experiences.

Our Intentions: As students critically read and analyze a variety of magazines, they will be asked to think about the purpose of this genre, its intended audiences, various design elements, and to use these understandings as a resource for constructing meaning. The more readers know about magazines, the more they will be able to read and comprehend them.

Lesson Overview: Using a *Ranger Rick* magazine and a variety of other magazines designed for young readers, we will construct a reading guide for approaching and comprehending magazines. This lesson highlights how and why we read magazines, and how the images and written texts position us as readers in particular ways.

Language of Instruction: Good morning, Readers! Last week, we looked at a variety of genres and analyzed the forms that each genre may assume. Today, we are going to look at a specific genre: children's magazines. In our classroom library, we have *Ranger Rick, Time for Kids, American Girl, Teen Magazine, Teen Vogue, Creative Kids Magazine, National Geographic Explorer, Boys Life*, and *Sports Illustrated for Kids*.

Let's begin by asking, "What do we know about this genre?" How many of you buy magazines or get them delivered to your home? Why do you read them? [*Discuss*.] As we can see by our discussion, we are all interested in the specific information that is included in the magazines we purchase. A magazine has a very specific audience, and is usually about a specific topic.

Like newspapers, magazines are much more timely than textbooks. The information in magazines is very current and usually quite relevant to the reader compared to textbooks, which can be more extensive and often outdated. In the magazines we have in the classroom, the writing is geared toward kids and has children's interests in mind.

Let's think a little about *how* we read magazines. For example, I know that skimming will be an important reading practice for the magazine genre. When we open a magazine, we might begin by looking at the photos, captions, or the table of contents to see what is in this issue. Then we can make decisions about what to read and what to skip. There are headings and subheadings just like a textbook or an informational text and so our skimming of a particular article might be very similar to skimming a textbook. We have also talked about reading advertisements (see Lesson 4.6). How do the advertisements affect your reading? Are you sometimes distracted by the ads, or is that why you read the magazine? Some of these magazines are written for educational purposes and do not have any advertisements, but the *Teen Vogue, American Girl, Boys Life*, and *Sports Illustrated for Kids* all have advertisements that really pertain to a particular audience (see Lesson 4.6).

Let's take a look at some of the images included in these magazines. Would you buy a magazine that was all text? Probably not. So images are an important feature in this genre. How do some of these images make you feel? Are there differences between images in an article and those in advertisements? What do the images do for us? [*Discuss.*] I think it is important for us also to analyze how children are portrayed in the magazine. What are the images of the children like? How are they dressed? Why do you think they are they included in the magazine? Do you feel like an insider or an outsider when viewing the images of them or reading the articles? (See Lesson 2.6.)

The reason I bring these ideas to your attention is because it is important not only to read and enjoy these magazines but also to take a step back and think about how the magazine makes you feel, and what the writers and publishers of the magazines expect. This activity will help you to understand the articles, and also strengthen your critical-reading skills.

I have a box full of other magazines for you to consider. Come up and choose one and use the guide we have created to examine your magazine selection (see Figure 4.10).

FIG. 4.10 *Strategies for Analyzing a Magazine*

> ❖ How do some of these images make you feel?
>
> ❖ Are there differences between images in an article and those in advertisements?
>
> ❖ What do the images do for us?
>
> ❖ What are the images of the children like? How are they dressed? Why do you think they are they included in the magazine?
>
> ❖ Do you feel like an insider or an outsider when viewing the images or reading the articles?
>
> ❖ How does this magazine influence me?
>
> ❖ What are the different reasons for reading a particular magazine?
>
> ❖ What is the purpose and usefulness of this magazine/genre?
>
> ❖ How does our background knowledge or interest in the topic impact our reading?
>
> ❖ What does my choice in magazines tell about me?

Mark any parts of the magazine with sticky notes that you would like to point out to the rest of the class. You might mark places of interest or an answer to a question on the chart paper. You might also make a few notes concerning how you read the magazine.

Instructional Trajectory: We expect to see readers attend to the features of this genre and use this knowledge as a resource for their understandings. The more they know about the particular features, structures, and audiences of the magazine genre, and understand their purposes for reading, the greater their comprehension. We hope to see young readers evaluating and beginning to understand how particular magazines position them, not only through the advertisements but also through the articles and images as well.

Classroom Artifacts: Small-group guide sheets can be created to steer students in their investigation of various magazines as well as a whole-class charts to be used for future reflection.

Closing Comments: Analyzing magazines and their possible functions in our classroom culture and society will help readers critically engage and comprehend these texts at a deeper level. Many times readers enter into the reading without realizing that particular magazines position them in particular ways and that a magazine is a cultural artifact. Analysis of magazines can help young readers to critically read as well as enjoy this unique and entertaining genre.

Reading Biographies

The Challenge: Biographies are an important genre in children's literature, read and written throughout most elementary and middle school classrooms. Biographies provide an opportunity for readers to interact with people who have made a difference all over the world. Authors of biographies write about everyday heroes, sports stars, movie stars, historical figures, and present them within their historical and present-day context so readers understand the influences surrounding their life choices. There are many wonderful children's biographies on the market today, and we should expose our students to a wide variety of biographies.

Our Intentions: We expect students to become familiar with the genre of biography and to learn to appreciate this genre and its unique features. At the same time, we would like readers to be able to evaluate and analyze biographies. Too often, biographies are read as "truth" and children need to realize they are an interpretation of someone's life written by someone else.

Lesson Overview: Through a whole-class read-aloud of *Martin's Big Words* by Doreen Rappaport (2001), students will become familiar with one example of a biography, the picturebook biography, and use this example to analyze other biographies. After reading aloud *Martin's Big Words*, students will get into small groups and read other picturebook biographies to discuss, evaluate, and analyze.

Language of Instruction: Good morning, Readers! Today I am going to read aloud the biography *Martin's Big Words* by Doreen Rappaport. This is a type of biography called a picturebook biography. In this type of biography, both the text and the illustrations work together to portray a person's life. There are some aspects of biography that I would like for us to consider as we read this picturebook. For example, we might want to think about the authenticity or the accuracy of the information included in the biography, the writing style, the design elements used, and how the book is organized.

Let's read and examine some of the aspects of *Martin's Big Words*. Before we begin reading, what do we know about the author and illustrator? We might want to look at author and illustrator notes to see if it tells us how much research this person has done or what relationship they might have had to the person. Did they receive any awards for this book and what might that tell us? [*Read author and illustrator's notes as well as the awards on the front cover.*] We might also look at the author and illustrator and consider who they are, what other books they have written, and what we know about that author, like their reputation. In this book, we see that both the author and illustrator have given us lots of information about how they researched Martin Luther King's life before they started writing, and on their organizational and design choices. This really helps us to read the biography, using these notes as sources of information. For example, we might not have known that the four candles in one illustration represent four girls killed in the Baptist church bombing. Without the information in the author and illustrator's note we might not have made any connections to that event. We also learned how and why Doreen Rappaport decided to use Martin Luther King's words to organize her picturebook. Now let's read the book and see how that information provided to us by the author and illustrator impacts what we think about Martin Luther King Jr. [*Discuss images and text during the read-aloud.*]

On this chart paper I have some other aspects of biographies that I would like us to consider. (See Figure 4.10.) We will use *Martin's Big Words* as an example and then in small groups we will read other picturebook biographies and discuss, analyze, and evaluate them just like we are doing now.

OK, now that we have discussed the criteria for biographies as well as our interpretations, I would like small groups to investigate one of the following picturebook biographies: *The Man Who Walked Between the Towers* (Gerstein 2003), *The Librarian of Basra* (Winter 2005), *When Marian Sang* (Ryan 2002), *Snowflake Bentley* (Martin 1998). After you have finished discussing these picturebook biographies, we will come back together and discuss their strengths and weaknesses.

FIG. 4.11 *Examining a Picturebook Biography*

❖ What are your initial impressions?

❖ What do we know about the author and illustrator?

❖ What is their reputation?

❖ What information is given in the text?

❖ What information is provided through the illustrations?

❖ What type of illustrations are included?

❖ What medium was used? Was it effective?

❖ How is the book organized?

❖ What is the style of writing used?

❖ How is the person portrayed?

❖ Are negative and positive aspects shared?

❖ Is it authentic and accurate? How do you know?

❖ Is it interesting?

❖ Did you make any connections to other biographies or books?

❖ Are there any unanswered questions?

Instructional Trajectory: This lesson will help students build an appreciation for biographies as they become aware of the variety available to read. In future lessons, other types of biographies could be introduced as well as evaluated and discussed in much the same manner. We expect to see children read and analyze biographies with the understanding that, even though extensive research has been conducted, biographies are an interpretation of a person's life constructed from various resources.

Classroom Artifacts: Classroom charts and small-group charts could be constructed to record students' discussions on each biography.

Closing Comments: Understanding the nature of biography is important for readers as they read and write this genre many times in their school career. Students are often assigned various biographies to read and are not given the opportunity to evaluate their effectiveness. Perhaps this lesson will help readers understand the important way that biographies provide opportunities to learn about other cultures past and present.

Comprehending Novels and Extended Texts

For most of our teaching careers, we have not used novels as a primary resource for the explicit teaching of reading and comprehension strategies. We have used what Ralph Fletcher calls *microtexts*, shorter texts like poems, picture-books, and short stories, for the introduction and demonstration of reading and comprehension strategies. Although novels have always been an integral part of our reading workshop—for example, read-alouds, independent reading, and most important, literature study groups—the strategies we demonstrate through explicit instructional lessons and think-alouds are done with texts that can be read in a single sitting.

How do we ensure that students apply the strategies we teach through these microtexts when reading novels independently and during literature study groups? The lessons in this strand highlight the procedures we use to help readers comprehend, discuss, and analyze novels and other extended texts. We will address some of the same strategies we used with shorter texts—for example, coding, creating class charts, and interactive discussion strategies—and we will also share some new methods that work better with extended texts, such as character evolution, comparing covers, and quotable quotes. These strategies are designed to help readers maintain their focus throughout a novel and deal with the level of complexity in these lengthier texts.

It is important to state at the outset that although we read novels aloud, during independent reading, and in literature study groups in the reading workshop, they are only one component of our reading workshop. We have never used, nor would we advocate the use of, a single novel for whole-class book studies, where every student has a copy of a particular novel and follows along during a round-robin reading activity. We have been unable to find any research to support this type of reading instruction, and the anecdotal evidence overwhelmingly suggests that this traditional, outdated mode of instruction is ineffective for developing lifelong readers that comprehend what they are reading. If students want to follow along with a novel as we are reading it aloud to the class, that is their choice and we allow them to do so, but it is not required. We want students to attend to the novel being read aloud, to follow along with the characters and events in the story; however, they can usually do this by sitting back and enjoying a tale well told.

Novel reading is not viewed as the ultimate goal of the reading workshop, with picturebooks relegated to some intermediary process to get readers ready for novels. Novels are simply one type of text that readers read as they progress through their lives. We want readers to find enjoyment and insight during their experiences with novels, but we also want them to continue to enjoy picturebooks, expository texts, web resources, short stories, poems, and other texts throughout their reading lives. Novels have an important part to play in our reading workshop, but they are not the only text required for reading.

The comprehension lessons in this section include:

5.1 Booktalks

5.2 Reflecting on Coding Patterns

5.3 Literary Gossip

5.4 Comparing Book Covers

5.5 Insiders and Outsiders with Novels

5.6 Intertextual Influences

5.7 Character Evolution

5.8 Quotable Quotes

Booktalks

The Challenge: Students need access to quality reading materials and some choice in determining what they read. However, choice and access are not sufficient. Students need to know what novels are available, listen to recommendations about what to read, and have time to explore the world of novels if they are to truly have choice in their reading lives.

Our Intentions: Making recommendations for students' reading requires teachers to expand their knowledge of children's literature and of the readers in their classes. Both types of knowledge are necessary for teachers to make insightful recommendations.

Lesson Overview: This lesson will focus on how to conduct *booktalks*, short advertisements to entice readers into selecting new titles, authors, genres, and topics.

Language of Instruction: Good morning, Readers! I just wanted to start the week off by letting you know about some of the new titles, authors, and illustrators that I have discovered lately. I also want to make you aware of some of the classic and award-winning books that are available in our classroom library, in the school library, or down the street at the public library. What I am going to demonstrate today is called a *booktalk*. A booktalk is a short advertisement for a particular book that tries to entice you to read the book, but doesn't give away enough information to ruin the reading. Later on, I will expect each of you to do some booktalks for the class so you can share some of your favorite books.

Let me give you an example. On of my favorite new books I have read this year is called *The Miraculous Journey of Edward Tulane* by Kate DiCamillo (2006). We have read other books by this author: *Because of Winn-Dixie* (2000), *The Tiger Rising* (2000), and *The Tale of Despereaux* (2003). In *The Miraculous Journey of Edward Tulane*, the main character, Abilene Tulane, has a china doll that she names Edward that gets lost while Abilene is on a cruise across the ocean. Edward is able to think, and describes what happens to him on the cruise and how he tries to get home to Abilene. If you like adventure stories and fantasy, you will probably like this new book by one of our favorite authors.

You see how I didn't give away the whole story, but just enough to tease you, to explain what the story is about, and to suggest who might like this kind of novel. That is the secret of a good booktalk, being able to entice readers without giving away the whole story and ruining it for them. I will do a couple more booktalks and then we can create a class chart describing what a quality booktalk involves.

Instructional Trajectory: The residual of these booktalks is simply the effect these advertisements have on students' selections and reading lives. Students, like all readers, often stay within a particular genre for a time before changing directions and trying new ones. The goal of booktalks is to get students to try books they might not have selected for themselves.

Classroom Artifacts: Booktalks can be collected with book reviews, publisher catalogs, and promotional materials to create a notebook for students to explore and find new books to read. A class chart describing what quality booktalks contain might look like Figure 5.1.

Closing Comments: Choosing a book for someone is a difficult task. The more you know someone, the better your chances of making a quality recommendation. Many readers, and unfortunately teachers, are not always aware of the wonderful books that have been published. This is understandable given the vast number of new titles published every year. Investigating the American Library Association website (www.ala.org) and reading review materials in publications like *Booklinks, The Horn Book,* and *The Reading Teacher* helps teachers keep up with the new titles that become available. Of course, a refresher course in children's literature at a university with a well-read and informed instructor can be highly beneficial as well.

FIG. 5.1 *Quality Booktalks*

❖ read title, author, publication date

❖ enough information to entice readers

❖ don't give away the story or ending

❖ tell which readers might like this book

❖ compare the book to others like it

❖ offer a "teaser" to get people to read it

Reflecting on Coding Patterns

The Challenge: To support literature study discussions, many teachers have been using sticky notes to help readers highlight portions of texts they feel are noteworthy and to bring ideas to their small-group discussions. In many classrooms, we have seen books filled with sticky notes (codes) containing students' highlights of various plot events, elements of literature, and responses or insights. One of the challenges has been figuring out what to do with these sticky notes—how to use them to support discussion, and whether they should be used as assessment devices.

Our Intentions: The focus of this lesson is on what to do with the codes after the book has been read and the discussion initiated. In order to support readers' reflections on what has been read and interpreted, we feel the codes need to be organized and analyzed to look for patterns that may reveal clues about the readers' reactions to a particular novel.

Lesson Overview: After students have used codes to highlight important aspects of a novel, we have students take their sticky notes or codes out of the novels and organize them into categories. These categories are then used as discussion points throughout the literature study discussion, rather than always focusing on individual codes.

Language of Instruction: Good morning, Readers! Today we are going to talk about the novels we have been reading in our literature study groups. More specifically, we are going to talk about the sticky notes we have been using to mark or code the text to highlight things we want to share and discuss when our groups meet. Have you noticed that I have asked you not to take any of the sticky notes out of the novels? Well, that's because we are going to do something with them. If you take a look on the board behind me, you will notice all the notes that came from my copy of the book *Bucking the Sarge* by Christopher Paul Curtis (2004). Let me read some of the things that I have written down on my notes. [*Read and discuss.*] Can you see if any of the notes might relate to other notes? For example, it seems that many of the codes I put in the novel refer to one of the characters named Luther. I could put all the notes about Luther in one section. Are there any other things that seem to fit together? [*Discussion*] I noticed that I coded the language that Christopher Paul Curtis used a lot. We could put those notes together as well. OK, you seem to get the idea here. So, here's what we are going to do. I have some chart paper for each of you. I would like you to go to a table and take the sticky notes from the novels you have finished reading and lay them out on the chart paper and see if you can find any patterns in your codes. I will walk around and help out.

Instructional Trajectory: The residual effects of this lesson will be realized in the discussions that take place in literature study groups. The goal is to use these reflection charts and the individual codes to support and expand the discussions we have about the novels under investigation. Using the codes as a starting point and by organizing them into categories, we are better able to reflect on the responses we had to a novel, the way we respond across novels, and to summarize and share some of our reactions to a text.

Classroom Artifacts: Students will generate individual charts of their own categories of codes and responses. These can take a variety of forms.

Closing Comments: The primary reason for this lesson was our observation time and again of students coming to literature study groups with books filled to the brim with sticky notes. Each student in turn would simply read from their notes, and in turn would be followed by another student, and then another. There was very little interaction about what had been written, and rarely any discussion of why certain things were coded. Remember: the sticky notes or codes are not an end in themselves—they are a vehicle to be used to help readers analyze novels and other extended texts. We need to be sure we keep this goal in our students' mind when we ask them to code texts.

Literary Gossip

The Challenge: Have you ever read an education article where your professor or someone has written down their ideas, responses, and reactions in the margin? It seems we are sometimes just as interested in how they responded as we are in the actual article. This notion prompted us to consider ways to get readers' "histories of readings" out in the open and to consider the implications for their ways of responding.

Our Intentions: This lesson focuses on the use of sticky notes as codes across readers. We want three readers to code the same text and share their codes with other readers as they read. By doing so, we hope to get readers to consider how other readers have reacted to a text, attend to what other readers have noticed, and use these interpretations and comments to expand their own thoughts about the text.

Lesson Overview: This lesson begins with having one reader read a novel and use sticky notes with short phrases on them to highlight things that interest him and that he wants to discuss later on. In general, we use shorter novels, for example, *The Islander* by Cynthia Rylant (1998) or *The Whipping Boy* by Sid Fleischman (1987), for this reason. After the first reader is finished reading and coding the text, she gives the novel with sticky notes still in the novel to another reader, who then reads the novel and places his additional codes (in another color sticky note) in the novel. This is repeated a third time until the book is given back to the original reader to look at the notes from the other two readers. The notes can then be used a starting point for literature study discussions.

Language of Instruction: Good morning, Readers! Remember our discussions recently about using sticky notes or codes to organize our thoughts and reflect on how we responded to a particular novel? Well, we are going to try a different twist on that lesson today. I have a collection of shorter, but still interesting and meaty novels here to share with you. I only have one copy of each novel, so we are going to share the same book among three readers. You might also notice that each book has three stacks of different colored sticky notes. Here's what we are going to do. Each person will get a different colored sticky note. One person will read the novel first and code the text in much the same way as we have before. Only this time you will give the novel with the sticky notes still inside to the second reader. Then, the second reader will do the same thing and pass the book to the third reader. Try not to let all the notes get in your way when you read, but keep them on the right page if you have to move them around. When all three readers have read and coded the text, we will meet and discuss how this went. This is sort of an experiment, so we will have to see how this works. It doesn't matter which reader goes first, second, or third. You can decide the order you read the novel. In a few weeks, we will take a look at what we did and how it affected our reading experiences.

Instructional Trajectory: In similar fashion to the ways we used the categories of codes in Lesson 5.2, we could take all of the sticky notes out of the novel and organize them into patterns across the three readers. Once again, the focus is on the process of reflecting on what has been read as much as the chart that is constructed.

Classroom Artifacts: The artifacts are the codes from the novels, which can be laid out and organized in a similar fashion to what we did with the codes in Lesson 5.2. We believe these codes can be used to reflect back our reading and interpretations of novels. Charts with patterns of response could be created from the coded texts.

Closing Comments: We have called this lesson "literary gossip" because it is like readers gossiping about their ideas as they read a novel. One of the biggest challenges with coding texts is the interference that this may cause when reading. I have had numerous students explain how the posting of codes slows down their reading and makes them think about what they are doing. But that is the point! When we are reading for enjoyment or to escape into a story, yes, we agree that coding a text would interfere with our experience. However, reading for a literature study group is different. We want our students to have *both* experiences in our classrooms: reading for enjoyment or to get "lost" in a story, and reading to analyze and delve deeper into the author's craft and story. We believe there is a place for both types of reading in the reading workshop.

Comparing Book Covers

The Challenge:	As soon as a movie version of a novel is released, it seems that the cover of that novel is changed into a scene from the movie to entice readers to buy the book. Looking at an array of covers can offer new insights into the novel and how the publisher is marketing the book. The covers of books are reflective of the period in which the new cover is released. Artistic styles, content, and what characters are portrayed change depending on the marketing strategies of publishing companies. However, these changes may offer different clues to the reader about what is significant and what is to be attended to in the novel.
Our Intentions:	After locating two or more versions of the cover of a particular novel, we will discuss how the illustrators and designers have interpreted the story and compare this with our class' interpretations. It is important for students to realize that the covers of books have as much to do with how they are marketed as they do with the actual story. In many cases, the author or illustrator has no say in how the cover is designed or what is included. Students need to know this when they are looking at covers and predicting what might happen, or what the book is all about.
Lesson Overview:	Using several versions of the covers of a particular novel, students will discuss what is being portrayed and how that aligns or conflicts with their interpretations of the events, characters, and setting of the novel. They will also be asked to consider why the covers may have changed.
Language of Instruction:	Good morning, Readers! Have any of you noticed how the covers of novels change sometimes? I have here two different versions of the novel *Tuck Everlasting* by Natalie Babbitt (1975), and three different versions of the novel *The Whipping Boy* by Sid Fleischmann (1987). Let's begin by discussing the covers of *Tuck Everlasting*. The yellowish cover with the house and the woods is the original paperback cover and this one with the two people on it is the cover that came out after the movie of the book was released. Can anyone tell me why you think they change covers like that? [*Discussion*] The original cover looked more like a piece of art while the new cover looks more like a still shot from a movie. Why might the publishers do that? [*Discussion*] Another example is the three versions of the novel *The Whipping Boy* by Sid Fleischman. The first cover was designed by Peter Sis and his name is listed on the cover as the illustrator. Peter Sis also did the black-and-white sketches that are included in every chapter opening. The other two covers look more like movie posters or cartoon

characters. I wonder why the publisher changed this cover so many times. [*Discussion*] What effects do the different covers have on you as readers? What is contained in the new covers that was not contained in the older ones? It is interesting to see how the size and placement of characters has changed in the covers of *The Whipping Boy* over time. Let's see if we can find any other novels with different covers. We need to consider why this is done and what it offers us as readers.

Instructional Trajectory: Since the practice of creating multiple covers seems to be growing, we will have numerous opportunities to do this with new covers of various novels. The goal of this lesson is to challenge the idea that what is on the cover is what the author imagined, or what readers are supposed to visualize.

Classroom Artifacts: Making color copies of a series of book covers allows for students to revisit what has been discussed and further analyze the designs in the future. The covers could be displayed in a timeline so students could consider the period in which the new covers were released.

Closing Comments: Although this may at first seem like a rather simplistic lesson, understanding that children's literature is also an economic commodity that is marketed, advertised, and sold in large quantities is an important realization for many novice readers. Illustrators are paid handsomely for their art and cover designs, and teams of graphic designers, marketing directors, and sales managers spend a great deal of time deciding what art, graphics, fonts, and language to include on the covers of novels. It will be interesting to watch and see what happens to the covers of the Harry Potter series as it moves into paperback and other versions.

Insiders and Outsiders with Novels

The Challenge: During the course of a novel, readers encounter characters, settings, and storylines to which they can immediately relate, and other characters and settings that seem foreign or unfamiliar to them. Reading as an *insider*, someone who has had similar experiences to the characters in the story, or as an *outsider*, someone who cannot directly relate to the events and experiences in a story, poses different challenges to readers.

Our Intentions: This lesson will focus on two perspectives readers may experience as they read a novel, which we are calling insider and outsider perspectives. The goal is to understand how these stances differ and how they can affect one's reading and interpretations.

Lesson Overview: Using different novels that students are acquainted with, this lesson focuses on how one reads a novel as an insider or outsider. As students read novels there are times when they can closely relate to the events or characters' predicaments in the story, and times when they are positioned as a voyeur, watching events unfold as an outsider, unable to directly relate to the things the characters are experiencing. Each stance requires a different way of thinking to be able to comprehend the story and reflect on one's own responses to the events contained therein.

Language of Instruction: Good morning, Readers! Have you ever read a novel and felt like you had been through the same situations and challenges as the main character? Then, there are times it seems like you can't relate at all to what is happening. [*Discussion*] Well, we are going to refer to this as the difference between being an insider, and an outsider. Let's take a minute and discuss the differences between these two perspectives. When we are positioned as an insider, we understand what the character is feeling and can directly relate to what they are going through. Sometimes we feel like an insider because the character is the same age, gender, race, ethnic background, or lives in the same place or situation as ourselves. When the circumstances the character experiences are different from our own experiences we can feel like an outsider when reading a novel. We don't understand what they are going through and don't know how we would react in the same circumstances.

Last week, I remember a few boys saying that they couldn't get into the story we were reading because the main character was a girl. This is an example of what I mean by being an outsider. It doesn't mean we have to stop reading the book because we aren't the same gender as the main character. I read books with female characters all the time. But, it does mean that we will be experiencing the book in different ways than if the character was more like ourselves and had similar experiences. Besides, just because the character is a different gender doesn't mean you won't be able to relate to what they are going through. Many times boys and girls experience similar things growing up.

As an outsider, we sometimes have trouble understanding why characters react the way they do, and why they think the things they do. This can make it a challenge to understand the events in a novel. In order to get through this challenge, we have to first recognize when we feel like an insider or outsider. I am going to read several passages from some of the novels we have been reading and we are going to discuss whether we feel like insiders or outsiders and how this affects our interpretations. As I am reading, consider when you feel like you can relate to the setting or characters, and the times when you are uncertain about what is happening. We will then talk about how we deal with these two perspectives.

Instructional Trajectory: Understanding one's stance or perspective and how this affects one's interpretation is as important as any lesson we teach. Literature discussions should be affected by this lesson and there should be evidence that students are attending to the readers' perspective in their reader-response notebooks. Trying to understanding the events from another's perspective is an important skill for novice readers.

Classroom Artifacts: An Insider–Outsider chart is one possible artifact. Students can list times during a story when they feel like either an insider or outsider and these can be collated into a class chart. However, since this distinction depends on personal responses, whole-class charts are often problematic. Another artifact can be lists of books that students create in their response notebooks focusing on times when they are insiders or outsiders.

Closing Comments: Reading a novel from an insider's perspective is very different from reading as an outsider. When one can relate directly to the events a character goes through, or the thoughts that characters share, the reader is able to make more personal connections, empathize with the character's plight, and possibly anticipate outcomes and turn of events. As an outsider, we learn about the character in a secondhand fashion. Some educators have referred to this as the "literature as mirror, literature as window" phenomenon, where we see through the window of literature into the lives of others, and into our own lives through the mirror of literature. Both perspectives are important aspects of our experiences with literature. Literature illuminates our own lives and the lives of the characters we meet in literature.

Intertextual Influences

The Challenge: One of the most challenging aspects of conducting a multiday literature study group discussion is sustaining interest and depth of the interpretations beyond the first conversation. The initial discussion often focuses on "likes and dislikes" and addresses students' opinions of the quality of the story. Using sticky notes to code texts has helped students sustain discussions by going back to the text for specific references and events. However, the teacher is responsible for guiding the discussion forward and helping students select a focus for subsequent discussions. Bringing in other texts, picturebooks, poetry, or expository texts to help readers make intertextual connections and comparisons can extend the life and dimensions of a literature study discussion.

Our Intentions: By selecting shorter texts (poems, picturebooks, short stories, editorials, or articles) that are connected to the events, themes, character, and topics in the novel under study, teachers can extend and expand the possibilities of literature discussions. These intertextual connections help readers see associations across texts and genres and help them understand topics, themes, and events from a variety of perspectives.

Lesson Overview: Selected poems, picturebooks, and nonfiction articles are read alongside the novel being discussed. These shorter texts are interjected into the literature study group after the initial discussions of a novel. Waiting until after the initial discussions allows readers to establish some understandings of a particular novel before being asked to connect the novel to other texts.

Language of Instruction: Good morning, Literature Study Group Members! We have been reading and discussing a great novel called *The Boy in the Striped Pajamas* by John Boyne (2007) for the last few days. Our discussions have been going very well about the Holocaust and that particular time in the world's history. Today, I am going to ask you to read one of the picturebooks or poems that I have selected and think about the relationship between the novel and the texts I have brought to the group. I have selected these poems and picturebooks to enhance and extend our discussions. I'm sure once you begin to read what I give you, you will see the connections to the characters and events in *The Boy in the Striped Pajamas*, and will have lots to add to our discussion. You can use your reader-response notebooks to take notes on the picturebooks or poems that I share with you. I think you will find that the novel we read affects how we understand the picturebooks or poems, and these shorter texts affect how we read and understand the novel.

Instructional Trajectory: Making intertextual connections is a strategy that all readers employ whether we specifically select texts to make connections or simply remember other texts we have encountered. As the shared experience of a class grows with each new book read aloud, during independent reading, or in literature study groups, the basis for intertextual connections expands. The more connected the texts we read and share, the more connections will be made by readers.

Classroom Artifacts: Charts indicating the novel being read and all of the connected texts available for students to explore can be posted to allow students to read further into a specific topic or theme. A "novel web" centered around the novel with lines indicating connections to other books would support the connections made during discussions.

Closing Comments: In many middle and high school and even some elementary language arts curricula, there is a canon of literature (a sequence of required readings) that teachers are required to cover. Too often, these required readings are "classics" that students have difficulty connecting to and comprehending. When a single book, for example, *The Diary of a Young Girl* by Anne Frank (1991), is the only point of entry into a subject as complex as World War II or the Holocaust, many students fail to understand the context of the novel or have the requisite background knowledge to make sense of the events in the story. By incorporating other shorter, more accessible texts into the discussion, students can use those easier texts as points of entry into the subject matter, setting, or historical events, and find ways to connect to the work under study. We don't want a single text, novel or otherwise, to be the only point of entry into any subject or event.

FIG. 5.2 *Selected Picturebooks About Internment*

Rose Blanche—Roberto Innocenti

Baseball Saved Us—Ken Mochizuki

Home of the Brave—Allen Say

Let the Celebrations Begin!—Margaret Wild

The Butterfly—Patricia Polacco

So Far from the Sea—Eve Bunting

Character Evolution

The Challenge: Being able to describe the changes in a character throughout a novel is more important than being able to simply make a character web listing the characteristics of a particular character in the novel. The changes the character undergoes is one of the driving forces of a novel, propelling the reader forward into the storyline.

Our Intentions: By using a variety of strategies—for example, character interviews, fictional biographies, and autobiographies—and character sketches, this series of lessons will help readers attend to the way a character evolves during the course of a novel.

Lesson Overview: This series of lessons focuses on a particular character from a novel, in many instances the main character. Understanding the ways a character evolves requires readers to assimilate a variety of information, including the physical characteristics, actions, thoughts, and other characters' descriptions and reactions.

Language of Instruction: Good morning, Readers! We have all been reading novels during independent reading and in our literature study groups for some time now. I have been noticing in your reader-response notebooks and in our discussions that you have been getting pretty good at describing the main character in your books. However, I have noticed that you don't seem to be paying as much attention to the ways the characters evolve during the course of the novel. Can anyone tell me what *evolves* means? OK, so it means how the character changes during the story. For the next week or so we are going to incorporate a couple of new learning experiences into our discussions of the novel we are reading aloud, and then try them with some of the novels we are reading independently or in our literature study groups. The first experience is writing a biography of one of the characters. This biography would be fictional, of course, but you would have plenty of evidence from the novel to create a biographical statement about a particular character that would include information in the text or things you may infer from the novel. A second experience we might try is interviewing a character. You would pair up with someone; one person would be the character and one person would ask that character some questions. A third experience would be where we draw a picture of what we think the character looks like and put him in a setting that makes sense based on the story. To begin, let's take the character Liesel from our novel *The Book Thief* by Markus Zusak (2006). What might she look like, or what might she say in an interview? Let's create a class chart listing some of the questions we could ask a particular character. We need to be sure we consider how Liesel starts out in the book and all the changes she undergoes throughout this novel.

Instructional Trajectory: Attention to character is an important consideration in many of the young adult novels we read. As these lessons begin to have an effect, students will begin to notice how characters change, why they change, and how this affects the story they are reading. Character timelines can also be used to represent change over time. These ideas become the foundation for all subsequent discussions about character.

Classroom Artifacts: The interviews, biographies, and character sketches become artifacts to revisit and consider as readers explore new novels. A list of possible questions to ask a character is contained in Figure 5.3.

Closing Comments: These lessons are best demonstrated with a novel read aloud and then extended into independent reading and small-group discussions. The strategies we have described are only vehicles for helping readers think about characters in more complex ways. In other words, the goal is not to get good at creating character webs; the goal is deeper comprehension of the novels we read.

FIG. 5.3 *Possible Questions to Ask a Character*

> ❖ Why did you respond to the event the way you did?
>
> ❖ What was your childhood like?
>
> ❖ Who are your true friends?
>
> ❖ Who are your enemies?
>
> ❖ What makes you happy or sad?
>
> ❖ Why do you dress the way you do?
>
> ❖ What do you think will happen in your life after the story is over?
>
> ❖ What was happening in your life before the story began?

Quotable Quotes

The Challenge: Readers learn a great deal about characters and often about themselves by listening carefully to what characters say. As readers, we often remember and use famous quotes from the books we have read. How these quotes reveal characters' motives, personalities, and values is often overlooked by novice readers.

Our Intentions: By selecting specific quotes from a variety of novels, we demonstrate how what characters say provides a window into their psyche and a mirror into our own experiences and lives. Quotes are often used to explain things we cannot put into words ourselves.

Lesson Overview: Teachers and students will use their reader-response notebooks to keep track of specific quotes from an assortment of characters throughout the novels they read. These quotes then serve as a foundation for our literature discussions. Taken out of context, these quotes don't mean as much, so it is important to include notes about who offered the quote, the context in which it occurred, and one's initial interpretations.

Language of Instruction: Good morning, Readers! Have you noticed that I am always quoting other people? I love sharing quotes from certain books, television shows, movies, song lyrics, and other texts. Sometimes other people say things in ways that I wish I could. I like the way authors and other people put things so I simply take their words and make them my own. Of course, I always give credit to the original author when I use them in my writing or when I am trying to make a point verbally. Since they weren't my own words, I have to give others the credit. If you look at many of the novels we have read, authors sometimes use a quote to open a chapter. When quotes are used this way they are called *epigraphs*. Let's take a look at a couple of novels where authors have used quotes to open their chapters or to make a point in their writing. In the books *King Dork* by Frank Portman (2006) and *Godless* by Peter Hautman (2004), the authors use quotes to tell their stories and reveal insights into their characters. In another novel we have read and enjoyed, *Bud, Not Buddy*, Christopher Paul Curtis (1999) uses quotes to help us get to know the main character Bud, in the form of Bud's "Rules and Things." These quotes and rules are presented to us throughout the novel to allow us to understand how Bud sees the world. It can be a very effective writing technique. As we are reading, I think it is a good practice to keep track of relevant things that characters say in the story. I would like you to go back into any of the novels you are reading and copy down three or four quotes that you feel are revealing, things that help show significant features of your characters, or ones where you just like the way they sound. Tomorrow, we will share some of these quotes and discuss their importance. Be sure to include the page number, who said the quote, and a few notes about what was happening. It is important to know the context of a quote to better understand what it might mean.

Instructional Trajectory: Readers may begin to offer quotes as evidence of interpretations during literature study group and read-aloud discussions. The focus is not simply on the quote, but what the quote suggests about the characters, the setting, and the events in a particular story, as well as connecting the quotes to one's life and experiences.

Classroom Artifacts: The class may make a bulletin board or chart of favorite quotes to post in the classroom. Individual readers may also begin keeping lists of quotes in the reader-response notebooks.

Closing Comments: What characters say is a window into their thinking, personalities, values, and identities. By keeping track of a variety of quotes from particular novels, readers construct insights into the types of characters that have had an influence on their reading lives.

Critical Reading in the Social Sciences

In many elementary and middle school classrooms, the social sciences are being either pushed aside or integrated into the reading curriculum. The reading that students engage in during lessons in social studies is mainly geared toward extracting historical information, for example, dates and places, and finding the main idea of a selection rather than interpreting information and history from a variety of sources. Historical documents and accounts are always written from a particular perspective. The lessons in this strand are designed to help readers see the constructed nature of historical documents and historical fiction as a genre. It is important for teachers to provide a variety of perspectives and interpretations so students can gain a multifaceted perspective of history and other social phenomenon.

In order for students to see themselves as part of the history they read, they need the skills to read critically and to have an opportunity to engage in historical thinking across multiple resources. In addition, the lessons in this strand will help teachers and young readers to interact with multiple genres and modalities while expanding their reading repertoires and providing new avenues for interpreting historical texts and visual documents.

The comprehension lessons in this section include:

6.1 Approaching Primary Source Documents

6.2 Examining Primary Source Document Photographs

6.3 Analyzing and Creating Expository Texts

6.4 Analyzing Historical Fiction

6.5 Reading for Debates About Historical Events

6.6 Student Think-Aloud Clubs

6.7 Think-Aloud Comparisons

6.8 What Is NOT in the Book?

Approaching Primary Source Documents

The Challenge: Primary source documents are used in many intermediate and middle grade classrooms to enhance students' knowledge of a variety of topics in the social studies curriculum. Students need to understand that these images and texts were created in a particular context, for a particular reason, and were probably not originally intended to be used for instructional purposes. It is important to guide students' analysis and understandings of these source documents to better utilize them as resources for understanding historical events.

Our Intentions: The instructional experiences introduced in this lesson will enhance students reading and interpretation of primary source documents, and help them learn how to approach, analyze, and interpret these documents while considering their historical contexts.

Lesson Overview: In this lesson, we will use primary source documents from World War II to demonstrate how to approach and analyze these historical documents. We offer a series of questions for students to consider as they read these texts and we demonstrate how readers consider the perspectives used in creating these documents.

Language of Instruction: Good morning, Readers! Today I am going to read you Executive Order #9066 issued by President Roosevelt in 1942. This executive order resulted in the relocation of hundreds of thousands of Japanese Americans to internment camps throughout the United States during World War II. Before I read the document, let's considering the following questions to enhance our understanding of this primary source document and activate our prior knowledge (see Figure 6.1).

FIG. 6.1 *Questions for Approaching Primary Source Documents*

What was its date, and what was going on at that time?

What is the genre?

Is there anything unique about its appearance?

Who is the intended audience? What do we know about them?

Who is the author? What do we know about them?

How did we get the primary source document? What meaning does that have?

Where was or how was the original published or displayed?

FIG. 6.2 *Analyzing Primary Source Documents*

Why was the document written? Is there anything in the text to help you determine this?

What is the purpose and motivation of the order?

What was life like before and after the executive order was created?

Who does this affect?

How does this document compare to other documents created during WWII?

Does this document go along with other readings you have done on the topic?

Now, I am going to read Executive Order 9066. [*Read document.*] On the chart behind me, I have written some additional questions to consider now that we have read the document (see Figure 6.2).

Now that we have discussed some of the questions I provided, you have all been given a copy of the executive order to further consider in small groups. This will give you a chance to analyze those aspects we did not attend to in our whole-group discussion. Write down what you notice in the language, font, symbols, and other features of the document. Think about why this document might have been created. How does this document affect American history? What is the impact of this executive order on the Japanese Americans? Discuss the questions provided and we will meet again to consider your answers as a whole group.

Instructional Trajectory: By spending an extended amount of time on one primary source document, we hope students will use this as a model for approaching and analyzing other primary source documents. Even though the topics of the primary source documents will change and students may need additional guidance to understand the role these documents played in their historical context, this lesson will help them to approach primary source documents in the future and to learn to read, analyze, and critique the effects they had on historical events.

Classroom Artifacts: A classroom chart on how to approach primary source documents will be created, and students will be provided with an analysis guide to consider subsequent primary source documents.

Closing Comments: We think it is critically important that readers learn to understand the historical context of primary source documents and investigate the situation in which they were created. It is impossible to analyze and comprehend primary source documents without understanding the time period, people, and circumstances from which they were created.

Examining Primary Source Document Photographs

The Challenge: Throughout the social studies curriculum, students are asked to examine primary source documents, often including photographs, and are asked to make sense of them without the knowledge of how to approach a photograph as a historical document. Although photography is often considered an objective lens on reality, it is important for students to realize that photographs of any kind are not neutral representations of objective facts. Photographs, like historical texts, are created by interested parties. Analyzing these issues will help students look at photographs with a critical eye and to think about how and why the photographer may have chosen to represent a particular event in a particular way.

Our Intentions: We want students to think critically about photographs as primary source documents. To do this, we will demonstrate how to ask critical questions of these images, and look at them as a potential source of information. We also want students to realize that photographs are used to construct interpretations about the past, rather than as a view into the objective reality of the past.

Lesson Overview: Using a photograph from the Dorothea Lange collection of Japanese internment photographs from World War II, this lesson will help students to ask critical questions of a photograph, consider the context in which the image was captured, and analyze the varying perspectives of a particular photographer. This lesson is designed to call attention to the context and purposes surrounding historical documents, in particular photographs, and analyze how extending one's background knowledge can affect interpretations.

Language of Instruction: Good morning, Readers! Today I am going to give each of you a photograph taken from the collection of Dorothea Lange. She was a famous American photographer who took photos of the Dust Bowl and Japanese internment camps during World War II. On this chart are some questions I want you to consider as we look at the photographs (see Figure 6.3). Let's begin by asking ourselves what we see and notice when we first look at the photograph. I want you to only focus on what is in the photograph itself. Describe everything you see. Second, I want you to tell me what is not there. In other words, what questions might you have concerning what is not included in the photograph?

Next, I want you to use your knowledge of World War II, Japanese internment camps, and Dorothea Lange to make sense of the photographs I have provided. Consider the following questions: Why do you think this photograph was taken? Who might benefit

Noticings	What Is Not Included?	Interpretations

from this photograph? How does the photograph portray Japanese American internees? Does the photographer have a particular reason for portraying things in the photograph in a certain way?

Finally, let's look at some other photographs I have up here on the board taken by other photographers, including Ansel Adams and Masumi Hyashi. Compare and contrast these pictures with the photographs from Dorothea Lange. How do they differ? How are they similar? What is in the foreground? What is in the background? Why do you think there might be similarities? After you have had some time to consider and analyze these various photographs, we will gather back together and discuss our ideas.

Instructional Trajectory:

Guiding students to analyze and compare photographs helps them understand that photographs are not neutral representations of reality but were created with intention. Students will be shown how to apply this knowledge to historical photographs, as well as contemporary photographs included in magazines, books, and on the Internet. This lesson might continue by reading biographies on various photographers to get some background knowledge on why they chose to create these images and who hired them to create these photographs.

Classroom Artifacts:

Whole-group analysis of the Dorothea Lange photos will be charted and used as a reference for later discussions. Students will get into small groups and use the chart as a guide. These artifacts will be used throughout the year in other history units as a way of reflecting on their analysis of historical photographs.

Closing Comments:

Helping teachers and students to understand the nature of historic photography is very important as more and more primary source documents are used throughout the social studies curriculum. Asking critical questions encourages students to think about photographs as historical artifacts and as a resource to be used to construct interpretations about the past.

Analyzing and Creating Expository Texts

The Challenge: Students are expected to explore and comprehend expository texts with greater depth and frequency as they progress through the elementary and middle school grades. In addition, across all grade levels, there has been a significant increase in the number of expository texts being used, whether these are textbooks, trade titles, or online resources. Helping children understand expository text structures and elements can enhance their comprehension of these texts. Making connections between reading and writing expository texts can be a way for students to consider and analyze these structures and elements, and these connections can help readers to better comprehend informational texts.

Our Intentions: The goal of this lesson is to help readers better understand expository texts by having them create their own. Students will learn to navigate their own expository texts and make decisions about the elements and structures that best fit the needs of their topic.

Lesson Overview: Through the use of a write-aloud, we will demonstrate how to create an expository text about a particular topic. The write-aloud will make visible the thought processes that a proficient reader and writer might go through to construct an expository text. During the write-aloud the teacher will share her conscious decisions concerning the structure of the text, language choices, visual images, and graphic elements.

Language of Instruction: Good morning, Readers! During the past week we have been reading a variety of expository texts. Today, I am going to conduct a *write-aloud* to demonstrate how I would create an expository text for my research project on Yellowstone National Park. A write-aloud is where I sit and actually create the text in front of you and talk aloud about what I am doing as we go along. The reason I selected this topic is because I am taking a trip there next year and this information will be really helpful to me and my family. The first thing I need to determine is the content for my text. If I look at my research notes, I see that I have information on the animals I might see in Yellowstone, the Yellowstone River and hiking in Yellowstone, and where to stay and eat. I think for today's write-aloud I will begin with my notes on the animals of Yellowstone National Park. I will use two chart papers to serve as my first two pages, or a double-page spread, of my expository text.

Before I begin writing, I will need to brainstorm the important details that I want to include in the piece, and then decide what I want to present through images and what I want to present through written text. By looking through my notes, I have decided I will write about grizzly bears and wolves. I chose these because I am eager to learn more about these animals and I had quite a bit of information on them. My heading might say something about the two animals, like "The Two Most Popular Animals to See at Yellowstone." I think I will use one page for wolves and one page for grizzly bears. For wolves, I will have one section about the variety of wolf packs, and another on the history of wolves at Yellowstone. I will include a map of where the wolves are located and the names of the various packs found there. I also think I will include some pictures of wolves in their natural habitat interacting with each other. I have decided it is better to show this information using a map and some photographs than through written text.

In the section on grizzly bears, I want to include information about their daily habits within the park and what they eat. I think I will include a diagram showing the size of a grizzly bear compared to a human so that my readers get an idea about how big grizzly bears are. I also want some pictures of grizzly bears eating and interacting with other bears.

Before I begin writing the text for these pages, I have to think about the structure of this writing. Over here on the chart paper, I have included some examples of the different ways expository texts can be organized. We have read passages that were descriptive, compare and contrast, cause and effect, sequential, and question and answer. When you are constructing your text, you will need to decide which writing structures will best meet the needs of your information and your audience.

Once I get everything written and the photographs and diagrams organized, I need to decide on the layout. The layout of the page helps to guide readers on their reading path through the text and affects how they interact with the information. You will need to consider the layout of the pages as a resource for meaning as well. What do you want to include at the top? What text will be the largest, and what will be the smallest? Where will the pictures and photographs go? What is the most important aspect of your page that you really want your reader to pay attention to? I have decided I want my heading to be the biggest because that is what the page is all about. I want the captions to be smaller because most of the information is carried in the image. I have also decided I want the map of the wolves to be prominent. To make it stand out, I will place it in the center of the page because I consider that information to be the most fascinating aspect of my research on wolves.

The more we know about the types of expository texts that exist, the text structures within the texts, and the components of expository texts, the easier it will be to navigate and understand these often complex texts. OK, now it is your turn. Look at your topic and resources and chose only one page that you would like to work on and design your page taking into consideration all that we just discussed about reading and writing expository texts. Remember there are many more elements and components for expository texts; I only used what was important for my page. You have to determine what is right for your topic.

Instructional Trajectory: This lesson makes a powerful connection between reading and writing expository texts. Attending to the structures of expository texts will help children to understand how to navigate them and how the organizational structure will impact their reading. Future comprehension lessons will continue to highlight how the structures change with each text, and how the purpose of reading can determine the reading path.

Classroom Artifacts: Two charts were created, one to record the various kinds of organizational structures and another to highlight information to be presented in image and in text. In addition, an example of a two-page layout was constructed during the write-aloud.

Closing Comments: Expanding readers' repertoires for reading expository texts will help students become successful in their encounters with these texts as they progress through the grades. Understanding expository reading through writing also helps readers to gain insight into the texts they read and to think about the decisions various authors make, therefore helping them to be empowered critical readers.

Analyzing Historical Fiction

The Challenge: This lesson focuses on supporting students' reading of historical fiction. Reading historical fiction requires an understanding of the narrative elements of this genre and the ability to analyze the historical information included in the story. The challenge is to read and respond to historical fiction as a narrative, to empathize with the challenges the characters face, to be able to visualize the setting, and still be able to critically examine the accuracy of the historical information and the perspective the author adopts in telling the story.

Our Intentions: In this lesson, we want to help children read historical fiction through dual lenses: the literary qualities of the text, and the historical information being presented. Readers will come to understand that both historical and literary understandings are required to appreciate historical fiction.

Lesson Overview: We will read a historical fiction picturebook numerous times, looking at different features of the text during each reading. Students will research the historical information through a variety of resources and use this information to add to their initial interpretations.

Language of Instruction: Good morning, Readers! Over the next few days we are going to be reading the picturebook *Rhyolite: The True Story of a Ghost Town* by Diane Siebert (2003). We are going to look at this picturebook to understand the genre of historical fiction a little better, and to learn to respond to the historical, literary, and visual elements of this text. In the first reading through this book, I want you to feel free to discuss anything you notice or seems interesting. You might consider what you like or don't like, moments in the story that puzzle you, or connections of any kind you might have to the book. We will display our initial responses on a Noticings, Connections, Wonderings chart so we may refer to them over the next few days. [*Read and discuss.*]

Now that we have read the book and generated our initial interpretations, let's read it again and consider the textual and visual design elements. We will use a guide I created to help us examine this piece of historical fiction (see Figure 6.4).

Now that we have read the book twice and considered the textual and visual design elements, let's consider its historical contributions (see Figure 6.5). I am going to read the book again but I want you to think about how the book provides information about a ghost town in Nevada. We will add a historical information section to our chart. This will help us organize our ideas on the historical elements of the story.

FIG. 6.4 *Guide for Examining Historical Fiction*

May be copied for classroom use. © 2008 by Frank Serafini and Suzette Youngs, from *More (Advanced) Lessons in Comprehension*. Portsmouth, NH: Heinemann.

Personal responses to the text:

    Noticings:

    Connections:

    Wonderings:

Ideas about the text:

    Rhyme and rhythm:

    Symbols:

    Language:

    Story:

Ideas about the illustrations:

    Color:

    Line:

    Space:

    Shape:

Media used:

Ideas about the interplay of text and illustrations:

    How did the text and images work together?

    What information was included in the text?

    What information was included in the illustrations?

FIG. 6.5 *Examining Historical Evidence in Historical Fiction*

List some historical details.

Are these details accurate based on your other research?

What is the setting? Is it described accurately?

Who are the various characters? Are they portrayed accurately?

What does this book tell us about that time in history?

What is the author's perspective? Is this logical?

Now that we have read and analyzed the book for its literary and historical qualities, I would like you to meet in small groups to read some additional information on Rhyolite, Nevada. Each group has either a website or a book on Rhyolite and a copy of the picturebook. After researching the town of Rhyolite, I would like you to read the picturebook one more time coding the book with stickies. Code your ideas on the text, illustrations, history, and how all three work together. We will come back as a whole class and share our new insights.

Instructional Trajectory: This lesson is a great way for students to look at the literary, illustrative, and historical qualities of historical fiction picturebooks. Once students go through this in-depth investigation, they will be able to apply it to any picturebook they read, whether historical fiction, informational, or fantasy. We hope to see evidence of this understanding in many of their future literary responses.

Classroom Artifacts: A class picturebook analysis and personal picturebook analysis can be created. Students will also have the stickies in the books that can be shared and put together for comparison.

Closing Comments: Historical fiction picturebooks are very complex, as they require the reader to take in the illustrations, text, *and* historical features of the book and the time in history. Many times teachers use historical fiction books as a tool to teach history, and students rarely get to experience the aesthetic qualities of the text. Through this type of investigation, readers will analyze and understand many of the features of historical fiction.

Reading for Debates About Historical Events

The Challenge: Children are inundated with questions on a daily basis. Core reading programs and teachers themselves create numerous questions for assessing comprehension, or as a way to control the flow of classroom discussions. If we want students to act and think like historians then we need to guide them in the work of real historians, especially involving them in asking in-depth historical questions.

Our Intentions: This lesson is designed to strengthen students' reading and analytical skills as they consider important topics and essential questions concerning historical events. Students will formulate their own positions on key historical events and debate these ideas with other students.

Lesson Overview: At the end of a unit of study focusing on Japanese internment in America, readers will construct questions for a debate. Students will consider three types of questions that will lead to engaging discussions. In addition, students will be asked to conduct research in preparation for this debate, considering a variety of resources and guides to organize their thinking.

Language of Instruction: Good morning, Readers! Today we are going to work on creating questions for our debate on a historical event. We have been studying Japanese internment for the last few weeks and to bring closure to our unit of study we are going to have a discussion in response to what we have learned. As a class we are going to construct some questions together and then read and conduct research to prepare for the debate. To begin, we need to review the major aspects of Japanese internment that we have learned and see if we can create some interesting and thought-provoking topics for discussion (see Figure 6.6).

Now that we have reviewed many aspects of Japanese internment let's create some essential questions to think about and research (see Figure 6.7). We will have to consider three kinds of questions. Let's begin with some factual questions. These kinds of questions are about some of the facts that we have encountered and can locate answers directly in various resources. Sometimes these are called literal questions because the answers are literally in the text. Second, we can create analysis or interpretative questions. When you write these kinds of questions you might ask how or why something happened, or you might ask for an opinion about a particular topic. In order to answer these questions, it will be necessary for you to form an interpretation based on the

FIG. 6.6 *Possible Topics for Discussion/Debate on Japanese Internment*

- Immigration laws
- Japanese immigration to the United States
- Life before World War II
- Nisei and Issei
- President Roosevelt
- Executive Order #9066
- Comparison to other groups that have been denied citizenship
- Life in the internment camps
- Life after the internment camps
- Similarities to current events
- Children's literature about Japanese internment
- Bombing of Pearl Harbor

information we have available. The answers for these questions are not right in the resources; rather, they need to be constructed based on your readings, experiences, and perspectives on Japanese internment. Third, we can construct inferential questions. These questions go beyond the text and connect our thinking to the world, ourselves, or other historic events.

I will give you an example of each type of question, and then with a partner you will create two for each type and then record them on a chart. When we are done we will look at all the questions and decide which ones will support our discussion and debate.

Now that we have some questions to choose from, we will pick two or three from each section to become our essential questions for our debate. The word *debate* means that you will research your ideas on these questions and be prepared to defend your position. You will defend your position based on the texts that you read, personal experience, interviews with others, and any other resources we make available. You will need to use as many resources as possible. We have Internet sites, textbooks, informational text, picturebooks, historical fiction novels, video clips of Japanese internees, documentaries, and movies available here in the classroom. One way to organize your research is to think about the question and write down all that you know about your answer and then write down what you need to know (see Figure 6.8).

Let's use this guide sheet to help us prepare for the debate and to organize the information we have gathered. Next week, I will organize the class into groups and help you prepare for the debate.

Instructional Trajectory:

This lesson will influence inquiry projects that students undertake in the future as well as affect and enhance their research skills. Creating, answering, and debating the facts are lifelong skills that we want students to become proficient at and to use independently as they engage with other projects throughout the year.

FIG. 6.7 *Essential Questions Concerning Japanese Internment*

Factual Questions:

❖ What were the immigration laws before 1942?

❖ How did immigration laws impact Japanese internment?

❖ Why were Japanese Americans denied citizenship?

❖ What was life like in the camps?

❖ Who decided to detain Japanese Americans?

❖ What was life like before the war for Japanese living on the West Coast?

Interpretation and Analysis Questions:

❖ What was the impact of the Japanese attempts to prove their loyalty before, during, and after the war?

❖ How did Japanese internees cope during their internment?

❖ Are there differences in the texts written by Japanese and those written outside the culture?

❖ How do the words used in government documents compare to those used in texts written by Japanese Americans?

Inferential Questions:

❖ How are Japanese Americans and Native Americans alike?

❖ Does racism have an impact on your life today?

❖ What are the similarities and differences between the bombing of Pearl Harbor and the attack of the World Trade Center?

❖ How do concentration camps and internment camps compare?

FIG. 6.8 *Guide Sheet for Preparing for a Debate*

Selected Essential Question: What was the impact of the Japanese attempts to prove their loyalty before, during, and after the war?

1. What do I already know about topic?

2. How do I feel about this question?

3. Questions I have about the topic and question?

4. What are some different viewpoints on this question?

   U.S. government?

   U.S. citizens?

   Japanese citizens?

   Other citizens?

5. What resources do I need to answer this question?

6. Possible responses for the debate:

Classroom Artifacts: Classroom charts of topics and questions can be posted for future reference. Also, teachers can post the sample question and answer to serve as an example of how to read for this type of historical investigation.

Closing Comments: It is essential for students to become critical thinkers and producers of new knowledge if they are to see themselves as stakeholders in the future. Understanding that history is an act of interpretation rather than a set of facts to memorize will help them to begin the work of historians as they consider multiple perspectives and empathize with various historical groups. Asking essential questions that lead to inquiry will provide opportunities for students to read and write for authentic purposes.

Student Think-Aloud Clubs

The Challenge: Making our reading processes visible through think-alouds is a reading strategy that can greatly enhance comprehension. It slows the reading process down, helps readers to think about the strategies they use, and requires them to reflect on why they are reading. Reader comprehension can be enhanced as students become cognizant of their reading strategies through thinking aloud during the reading of expository texts.

Our Intentions: It is the goal of this lesson for students to become aware of the content of the texts they are reading and how reading influences their historical or scientific understandings. This lesson involves students learning to articulate their thoughts and interpretations of a content-area text, and to negotiate these insights with a small group of readers—a *think-aloud club*.

Lesson Overview: This lesson will begin with a teacher-directed demonstration of a think-aloud, and continue with students working with a partner or in small groups to construct their own think-alouds in response to a historical fiction picturebook.

Language of Instruction: Good morning, Readers! Today, I am going to demonstrate a think-aloud with the book *So Far from the Sea* written by Eve Bunting (1998) and illustrated by Chris Soentpiet. During this think-aloud, I am going to demonstrate how I approach and read the text, and how I consider the images in the picturebook to learn about World War II and the conditions of the Japanese internment camps in this story. I will use sticky notes to mark my thinking points as I read the text. As I am demonstrating the think-aloud, I want you to attend to what I do so that you can try to conduct a think-aloud in your groups.

After I have finished, you will choose a picturebook about World War II and begin by trying a think-aloud by yourself, placing sticky notes in your text to highlight your thinking points. After you have completed your individual think-aloud, you will read the book with a small group of students performing your think-loud. As a group you will then discuss each book you have selected in your small group. At the very end we will discuss all the books as a whole class. As you work on your thinking points, you should become aware of the reading strategies that you use, and how you use all the images and textual elements to make meaning with the text.

Let me begin by demonstrating what I mean as I think aloud while reading the book *So Far from the Sea*. To begin, I know this picturebook is an example of historical fiction about Japanese internment. On the book jacket, it states that Laura is visiting her grandfather's grave at Manzanar for the last time. This tells me it is a flashback story because it mentions that her father tells her the story of his relocation, and that helps her to know what she wants to leave on her grandfather's grave. Looking at the cover, I can tell they are in modern clothes, not the clothes they would have worn in 1942. All of this written and visual information helps me understand how Eve Bunting and Chris Soentpiet are going to tell the story. They are going to use a family's visit to remember that specific time in history. This is very different than *The Bracelet* by Yoshiko Uchida (1993), because that story is told *during* the time period in which it takes place, rather than as a flashback or a personal memoir. This book might also describe how Japanese internment affects the internee's descendants today, which is very interesting to me.

As I turn the pages, I realize that the flashbacks are illustrated in black and white and Laura's present-day story is in color. I am going to place a sticky on the picture of the classroom because it really helps me to understand how this camp turned into a small city as the character attempted to continue on with as normal a life as possible.

The sea and the boy's handkerchief might be used as symbols in this story. The sea may be used because Grandfather loved the sea and it was his home that he was taken away from and is now so far from. This is probably the inspiration for the name of the book as well. The neckerchief is from the dad's boy scout uniform. He put it on so he could look as American as possible, yet the irony here, too, is that it did not matter what he wore, what mattered was the color of his skin and his facial features. I am going to put a sticky note here on the neckerchief to represent the symbolism.

On the last page I am going to place a sticky note as well because Laura tells her father, "it was wrong," and her father replies, "sometimes in the end there is not right or wrong . . . it is just a thing that happened . . . a thing that cannot be changed." In this conversation the father tries to help Laura understand how he has come to terms with the past. In the picture the neckerchief is foregrounded with the wind blowing, making it look like a sail, representing the grandfather leaving Manzanar to go back to the sea.

I am going to place one final sticky note on the afterword. The afterword gives historic details about this story and helps us understand the context of the story. It is important to read all the parts of the book, as they are a resource for making meaning.

Now that I have finished demonstrating a think-aloud, let me ask you to discuss what you noticed about it. (See Figure 6.9.) What did I do as I read and created my think-aloud? [*Discuss.*]

Come and select one of the other picturebooks in our collection and go and create your own think-aloud. Use the sticky notes and mark your thinking points. You may use the class chart we just created, but as you are creating your think-aloud and you come across other reading practices that are important for understanding, keep them in mind so we can add them to the chart to make them available for other readers to consider.

Once the think-alouds are completed you will perform your think-aloud with your think-aloud club. You will read and discuss each book with three or four other readers.

FIG. 6.9 *Students' Responses to Teacher's Think-Aloud*

Read the book with interest and a good voice

Marked Noticings, Connections, Wonderings

Discussed and put sticky notes on the illustrations and title on the cover

Discussed the use of black-and-white and color illustrations

Shared ideas on the emotions of the characters

Made connections to other books and to historic information

Used background knowledge

Attended to the jacket for information and thought about how it helped you

Described how the author and illustrator were going to tell the story

Noticed symbolism and irony

Connected the book to our unit on Japanese internment

Your discussions can be about the book, how they tie into our history unit, or about the process of the think-aloud. The idea is that you are sharing your in-depth ideas with another group.

Instructional Trajectory: The construction of think-alouds will have a great impact on students' reading practices in future reading experiences. Think-alouds also help readers to be cognizant of the reading strategies necessary for reading a variety of content area texts.

Classroom Artifacts: A classroom chart with the think-aloud discussion notes and the think-aloud sticky notes within each picturebook.

Closing Comments: Individuals' reading strategies are supported as they think about their reading processes, what they notice and interpret, and share these ideas with other readers. The think-aloud clubs empower readers to articulate their interpretations of the text, and to share and negotiate within a small community of readers as they make their reading process visible.

Think-Aloud Comparisons

The Challenge: In many classrooms, teachers use think-alouds as an instructional tool to make the reading process visible. Think-alouds give children a chance to see how a proficient reader processes and organizes information during the act of reading. Often these think-alouds are used for a particular lesson and are not revisited to examine how they differ for reading various genres and for various purposes. It is critical for students to understand how to read a particular text, and how the reading process may change across texts and purposes.

Our Intentions: In this lesson, we want to show how looking back at various think-alouds for a variety of genres within a social studies unit provides an opportunity for students and teachers to go even deeper in their understanding of the reading process as well as the content-area topic.

Lesson Overview: This lesson is designed to help readers attend to the variety of reading strategies used as they move through different historical genres. We had completed a series of think-alouds prior to this lesson on the various genres students would meet in a study of the Iraq War. In this lesson, we compare and contrast the elements of each think-aloud and consider the reading strategies necessary for students' independent reading.

Language of Instruction: Good morning, Readers! On the wall behind me you can see the charts we have made that include ideas on the think-alouds that we previously conducted focusing on the Iraq War. We have think-alouds about an online news article, photographs, a presidential address, and a soldier's weblog. If you remember, I did a think-aloud to demonstrate the reading strategies needed to construct meaning for each of these texts or genres. On each chart we included the reading strategies used, and then asked the following questions (see Figure 6.10).

We are going to review these think-alouds and look at the similarities and differences across the texts, and discuss the different reading strategies and practices that are necessary to construct meaning with each. There will be some strategies that were used in all the think-alouds and there will be some that were unique to particular texts and genres. Let's begin by looking at the soldier's weblog. What are some similarities among other genres and what strategies are unique to reading this weblog written about the Iraq War? What reading strategies were used? How can we apply this knowledge to other weblogs and online publishing we might encounter in this unit? [*Discuss.*]

FIG. 6.10 *Think-Aloud Questions*

Who is the author?

What is the publication date?

Who is the intended audience?

What is the genre?

What are the characteristics of the genre?

What is the purpose of the genre?

What is the motivation for writing the piece?

In small groups, use the guide sheet and compare and contrast the other genre think-alouds and how they will help us to read and understand other readings we might encounter in our unit of study. When your group is finished, we will meet as a whole group to discuss our findings.

Instructional Trajectory:

Analyzing think-alouds across genres calls students' attention to the various reading strategies unique to particular genres, as well as those students might use across genres. This helps readers understand how reading strategies get applied based on the particular text being read, the purpose for reading, and the context of the reading event, rather than as a universal set of strategies to use with any reading selections.

Classroom Artifacts: Artifacts include the student guide sheet and a large classroom chart of the think-aloud comparisons (Figure 6.11).

FIG. 6.11 *Comparing Genre Think-Alouds*

Iraqi War Genres	Similarities Across Texts	Unique to the Text	Reading Strategies Used	How Might This Influence Our Future Reading
Soldier's Blog				
Presidential Address				
Online News Articles				
Photos				

Closing Comments: Guiding students to compare and analyze teacher think-alouds provides opportunities to understand how a proficient reader reads a particular text, and how to compare strategies across genres, purposes, and audiences. Think-alouds are effective demonstrations of how readers apply strategies and how these strategies support comprehension of particular genres.

What Is NOT in the Book?

The Challenge: For obvious reasons, most response strategies have focused on what is contained *in* a particular text. However, equally important is what is *not* contained in the written text and visual images, whether it has been intentionally omitted, and how this might affect our interpretations.

Our Intentions: By calling students' attention to events, information, and issues not included in an expository text, we can extend students' responses to additional resources and information that may add to their understandings.

Lesson Overview: Using several well-written expository texts across science, social studies, and other content areas, we will ask students to consider some things that have been left out of these texts. Using a series of questions, this lesson will ask students to make connections to their lives, background knowledge, and experiences to consider alternative possibilities.

Language of Instruction: Good morning, Readers! Have you ever noticed that there isn't a version from the Aboriginal or Native American perspective about Columbus, Cook, or another explorer's "discovery" of new worlds in our social studies textbook? Or have you noticed that when reading a science book about nuclear power, we don't see many examples of negative effects of these armaments? Another example: when we read about the Roman Empire, Egypt, or the Renaissance, we usually read about the wonderful art, philosophy, and lives of the kings, popes, and other rich and important people, and rarely hear about what life was like for the peasants or other disenfranchised populations. These are just a few examples of the things that are sometimes left out of the expository texts we have read and may want to reconsider. When we have talked about the books we have read, and I have asked you to respond to them, I usually ask you about things that are contained in the text. Not very often do we talk about things that have been left out. Well, today we are going to formulate some questions that we can ask ourselves that deal with things that may have been intentionally left out of a story or expository text (see Figure 6.12).

Let's take a look at the questions I have listed on the chart on the wall and consider how these questions might affect our interpretations and understandings of a particular text. Then we are going to choose a nonfiction picturebook we have already read and use these questions to reconsider what we learned.

Instructional Trajectory: Asking what is missing from a text is an important consideration, one that is too often neglected. In subsequent response notebook entries and class discussions, we would expect students to consider what is absent as well as what is included in the texts they are reading. If we are using notebooks in the content areas, one activity would be to list questions about the text that were not answered, people who were not included, perspectives that were missing, or information that seems contradicted by other sources. Only through the lens of multiple sources and perspectives do we get a more thorough and enlightened view of an event or issue.

Classroom Artifacts: The list of questions provided in Figure 6.12 will help students consider what has been omitted, intentionally or unintentionally, from a particular story or expository text.

Closing Comments: While interpretative process begins with perception, it may also begin with the perception of things *not* included in the text under consideration. This lesson calls students to look at what is outside the text: in other words, it requires readers to infer based on what is included in the written text and illustrations. Inferring is an important skill that requires readers to connect what is read with the experiences and knowledge of the readers' lives.

FIG. 6.12 *Questions for Considering What Has Been Left Out of a Story or Expository Text*

> ❖ Were there things left out of the illustrations that you thought needed to be included?
>
> ❖ Were characters or events portrayed in ways that were unexpected?
>
> ❖ What might you add to the story to make it more complete?
>
> ❖ Whose perspective was this text written from, and how did that affect what was included and what was left out?
>
> ❖ Do some research on the author and consider his or her perspective as it relates to the story.
>
> ❖ Who is portrayed in the illustrations and the text, and who seems to be missing?
>
> ❖ What do other sources of information say about the events, characters, and issues presented in this text?
>
> ❖ Is the information accurate and believable? Why or why not?
>
> ❖ Consider why the author or illustrator may have left certain things out, whether it was intentional or not, and how it changed your thinking about the story.

Comprehending Visual Images

As we go about our daily lives, we are presented with a vast array of visual and textual images, many of which affect the way we come to understand the world and ourselves. In today's society, visual images have come to equal, if not dominate, the modes we use to communicate and represent information in contemporary society. In how-to manuals, recipe books, websites, reference materials, advertisements, billboards, and the other texts in the lives of elementary, middle, and high school students, visual images have become more prominent, usually presented in *multimodal formats*. Unfortunately, these multimodal texts, texts that utilize a variety of visual and textual forms, have not been as prominent a feature in the language arts curriculum as they are in the lives of the students for whom the curriculum was intended.

Understanding visual images requires comprehension strategies and skills just as much as comprehending written texts. Particular comprehension strategies—for example, predicting, summarizing, inferring, and visualizing—often focus exclusively on written text. Given that many texts today are dominated by visual images, teachers need to be aware of the theories and practices involved with comprehending visual images, and develop techniques for teaching these to their students.

The lessons in this strand are based on the work of Gunther Kress and Theo van Leeuwen (1996), David Lewis (2001), Jane Doonan (1993), Carey Jewitt (Jewitt and Kress 2003), and other educational and literary theorists focusing on multimodal texts and analysis of visual elements. Their theoretical frameworks have provided a foundation for our lessons in comprehension and classroom instructional experiences. In these lessons, we have just begun to scratch the surface of these theorists' concepts and understandings. We strongly suggest that teachers take time to read some of the authors listed throughout this strand of lessons and expand their own understandings of visual elements and design.

Visual images are made up of many components. In these lessons we have included basic art techniques, perception theories, visual design analyses, and techniques for approaching and interpreting visual images by themselves and in the narrative sequence of the picturebook format. Understanding the artistic styles, choices, and components of individual images and the contexts in which these images appear, coupled with some discussion of the design and formatting choices of picturebooks, will expand readers' interpretive repertoires beyond written text.

The theories we present in this strand and the lessons that derive from them are commonly found in other disciplines like cultural studies, communication arts, sociology, and anthropology. Unfortunately, these concepts have taken too long to reach many educational theorists.

The comprehension lessons in this section include:

7.1 Approaching a Multimodal Text

7.2 Basic Elements of Visual Design

7.3 Considering Borders

7.4 Signifying Importance

7.5 Image Zones

7.6 Modality

7.7 Perspective and Viewing Distance

7.8 Artistic Styles

Approaching a Multimodal Text

The Challenge: The types of texts students experience on a daily basis have changed dramatically over the past ten years. Texts have become *multimodal*, meaning that they are comprised of written text, visual images, graphic elements, hyperlinks, video clips, audio clips, and other modes of representation. Helping students learn to navigate these texts and understand what the various components can do for the reader is an important aspect of the reading workshop.

Our Intentions: Different textual components require different reading strategies and comprehension practices. In order to understand these strategies, readers need to first recognize what is being offered in the text, and then to know how to navigate and make sense of the components.

Lesson Overview: This lesson is an introduction to the various images and textual components that readers may encounter in multimodal texts. Utilizing a variety of picturebooks, brochures, expository texts, magazines, and websites, this lesson is designed to help readers approach multimodal texts and understand the literary terrain before beginning to read.

Language of Instruction: Good morning, Readers! Have any of you noticed how different books are nowadays compared to the books you might have read when you were little? Let me show you some examples. [*Have several texts available that include various components and visual elements.*] Let's begin by making a list of the different modes that we find in these texts. There are many things we have to pay attention to when we read these texts. I think it makes it easier if you know the types of components and structures that are used in creating a book before you begin reading. Let me demonstrate how I approach one of these texts, thinking aloud about what I notice and attend to, then we will break into groups of two or three and you can try it yourselves.

Instructional Trajectory: Novice readers' comprehension will be expanded if they slow down and consider the components, structures, and design elements they may encounter in a text before they begin reading. Like many of the lessons in the book, teachers need to continue to demonstrate this way of approaching a text if it is to be effective.

FIG. 7.1 *Examples of Components of Multimodal Texts*

Peritextual Resources

❖ Endpages

❖ Dedications

❖ Covers

❖ Title pages

❖ Author notes

❖ Further information

Design Elements

❖ Borders

❖ Format—vertical or horizontal designs

❖ Placement of visual components (sidebars, graphics)

❖ Fonts

Illustrations

❖ Artistic style

❖ Full bleed, borders

❖ Use of the gutter

❖ Paper type

Classroom Artifacts: One chart generated during this lesson will be a Components of Multimodal Texts chart (see Figure 7.1) listing the various components students find in the books under examination. I have also included two charts that teachers can refer to and select various strategies for sharing with their students (see Figures 7.2 and 7.3). The components chart will relate directly to the books you select to analyze.

Closing Comments: Paying close attention to the various elements in a text is essential for increasing comprehension. We suggest that teachers spend approximately 25 percent of their time attending to or discussing the paratextual materials (e.g., all the elements in the picturebook outside of the actual story). When readers attend to the cover, endpages, author's notes, and other extra-textual materials, they are better positioned to make sense of the book they are exploring. Teachers need to explicitly demonstrate how to examine these extra-textual elements and what information is revealed by looking at these elements of a multimodal text.

FIG. 7.2 *Approaching a Picturebook*

Pick up the picturebook, looking specifically at its size, format (horizontal or vertical), and the materials used in construction (papers, graphics).

❖   Consider the author of the text and the artist. What media is used in the illustrations? What fonts are selected? Where is the text located on the page?

❖   Look at the cover, title, and illustrations. What expectations are set up for you as you approach the picturebook? What do the cover, title, and illustrations suggest?

❖   What is included in the peritext? The dedication, title page, author's note, endpages, and frontispiece?

❖   Skim through the book to understand the structure of the text. What is the overall structure of the book? Home-away-home? Repetitive structures or language? Cumulative? Chronological sequence?

FIG. 7.3 *Skimming a Multimodal Text*

Read through the picturebook more deliberately, marking important aspects you want to consider. After your second reading, consider the following questions:

❖   What were your initial reactions to the text and illustrations?

❖   How does the opening of the story compare with the closing of the story?

❖   How do the illustrations relate to the text?

❖   Words propel the reader forward and images slow the reader down. How did this tension between reading and viewing affect your experience?

❖   What kind of gaps does the author/illustrator leave for the reader to fill in? Are details purposefully left out to create tension?

❖   How does the story flow from page to page? Are there borders that separate things or does it cross over in language and image from one page to the next?

❖   Is there a relationship between form and content? Does the design of the book add to the content being presented? How?

❖   What themes were constructed as you read?

Basic Elements of Visual Design

The Challenge: Young readers may have been exposed to basic design elements in art class but rarely will they make the connection from these experiences to analyzing the art in picture-books. Several psychologists have written extensively about the "psychology of perception," including Rudolf Arnheim (1986), E. H. Gombrich (1961), and Donis A. Dondis (1973). Drawing on their theories will help readers understand how images are constructed and how artists represent emotions, meanings, and moods. This will help readers approach visual images, and understand some of the symbolic uses of color and basic visual elements.

Our Intentions: By introducing students to the basic elements of visual design, we will help focus their viewing and perceptions of what artists use to create their images, and give them a vocabulary to discuss images.

Lesson Overview: In this lesson, we introduce the basic elements of visual design and demonstrate how these elements are used by various.

Language of Instruction: Good morning, Artists! Yes, that's right, I said "artists," not readers this morning. I did that because today we are going to talk about art and visual design. We are going to take a look at how artists create their illustrations. There are a few basic elements (see Figure 7.4) that we need to know and understand and then we can look at some illustrations to see how artists use them in their work.

Let's start with the dot, the line, and the shape. A dot is a point in space, and a line is a dot that has moved in some direction. We have big dots and little dots. There are straight lines, angled lines, and curvy lines. Some lines are thick and some are thin. Lines are used to separate objects in an image, like the borders we discussed in our lesson about considering borders (Lesson 7.3). Lines may also show direction, like an arrow does. These lines point the viewer in some direction, like *leading lines* in a photograph. OK, now let's take a look at some shapes. There are three basic shapes that artists use: the circle, the triangle, and the rectangle or square. The square is thought to represent stability because it is a solid shape that doesn't have any diagonal lines. A triangle is thought to be more dynamic and unstable because the lines are slanted. The triangle represents action, motion, and sometimes tension or conflict. The circle has all curved lines and is thought to be warm and comfortable. Art theorists suggest the circle may also represent protection or safety.

Let's take a look at a new picturebook by one of our favorite authors Anthony Browne (2003). It is called *The Shape Game*. As I am reading the book, pay close attention to the shapes you see and let's talk about what basic elements of visual design Anthony Browne uses in his images. When we are done reading and discussing this book, we are going to explore some of the illustrations in a few of our other favorite books and discuss what we think these illustrators are doing with the basic elements of visual design.

Instructional Trajectory: Once these elements are demonstrated and discussed, it is up to the teacher to call upon them when exploring visual images in other settings. The purpose in this lesson is to give readers a tool for exploring and interpreting art. The art may be in picturebooks, on television, in galleries, or on a billboard.

Classroom Artifacts: Create a class chart of basic elements of visual design, including dot, line, shapes, and other appropriate elements (see Figure 7.4).

Closing Comments: We would suggest working with your art teacher to further explore these lessons. Hearing about these elements in different contexts may help to expand students' understandings of their purpose.

The understandings of visual elements that students develop are only worthwhile if they are used to explore visual images. Just knowing what a line is doesn't help if we don't know how and why it's used. However, this is not an exact science, in that these artistic codes and conventions raise possibilities, not definite meanings. Lines, dots, shapes, and textures can mean different things depending on the historical period, cultural context, and personal significance.

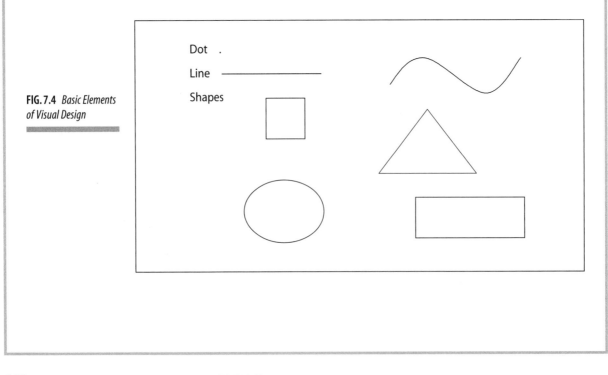

FIG. 7.4 *Basic Elements of Visual Design*

Considering Borders

The Challenge: Artists use borders and negative space (white space) to frame their images and draw readers' attention to the visual information in a variety of ways. Readers' perspectives change when looking at an image with heavy black borders as compared to looking at a full-bleed illustration, where the image extends over the whole page.

Our Intentions: This lesson is designed to help students understand how artists frame their illustrations. Attending to these visual elements is an important consideration when approaching a picturebook or an expository text. The way the image is presented can be just as important as what is contained in the image.

Lesson Overview: By examining a variety of visual images in picturebook illustrations, this lesson focuses readers' attention to where images are located in a picturebook, and the effect borders and visual space can have on one's interpretation of an image.

Language of Instruction: Good morning, Readers! Today we are going to take a look at a variety of illustrations in fictional picturebooks and some expository texts. Instead of looking at what is inside the images, we are going to begin by considering where the images are located in the book, whether the images have borders, how negative space or white space is used, and how this affects the meanings we construct. Let's begin with some of the images in Jon Scieszka and Lane Smith's (1994) book *The Book That Jack Wrote*. What do you notice about each illustration? [*Discussion about the frames around the pictures*] There are interesting borders or frames used to set off these illustrations. Notice how Smith breaks out of the frames in some images. Let's now take a look at the illustrations in *Smoky Night* by Eve Bunting and David Diaz (1994). Notice how Diaz used collage to frame the written text and how he used heavy, thick lines as borders around the images. Two other books we need to take a look at are *The Hello, Goodbye Window* by Norton Juster and Chris Raschka (2005), and *Officer Buckle and Gloria* by Peggy Rathmann (1995). Notice how the illustrators used white space rather than borders to frame their illustrations. Now here's the million-dollar question: "So what?" I'm not being snotty, but I really mean, "So what?" What do these different ways of framing illustrations do for us as readers? How do the frames affect our understandings and interpretations? The artists made these decisions for a reason. What do you think each one was trying to do? Let's talk about this for awhile and then we will analyze some of the other picturebooks we have been reading and see what other illustrators and picturebook designers are trying to do with the ways they position their images.

Instructional Trajectory: We are bombarded with images in a variety of styles and locations in our everyday lives. The goal of this lesson is to help readers carefully notice how images are presented, along with what is included in the image. These lessons should help students pay more attention to how images are located, framed, and presented regardless of whether they are encountered in picturebooks or on local billboards.

Classroom Artifacts: A chart listing the various ways that images are framed and some vocabulary for discussing images should be made available as a reference. We have created a list of questions that readers can use to ask themselves about the images they encounter in picturebooks.

Closing Comments: The ways that images are framed determine how we approach them. An image in a heavy frame suggests that we are looking through a window at the scene taking place. We are more detached and voyeuristic in our approach to the image. Full-bleed illustrations bring us in closer to the content of the image and create a feeling of being part of the action, rather than merely an observer.

FIG. 7.5 *Considering Borders and Design Elements*

❖ Are there borders around the illustrations or do the illustrations extend beyond all four sides of the page?

❖ How are the borders created? With lines, picture frames? Other designs?

❖ Is there any white space around the images? How is negative space used in the picturebook?

❖ Do you feel close to the images or distant?

❖ What style is the illustrator using?

Signifying Importance

The Challenge: Artists use various tools, elements, and techniques to draw viewers' attention to particular aspects or objects in their images. Understanding these techniques that signify importance is a vital step in learning to interpret visual images. Readers and viewers need to learn to attend to what is foregrounded and positioned as important, and what is backgrounded and considered less important as they explore various texts, illustrations, and genres.

Our Intentions: This lesson is intended to call students' attention to the various techniques that artists use to signal aspects of their images that they want viewers to pay close attention to. Various foregrounding and backgrounding, focusing, and positional techniques will be demonstrated.

Lesson Overview: Drawing on various images from magazines, picturebooks, and expository texts, teachers will discuss and call students' attention to the various techniques used to signify importance in visual images.

Language of Instruction: Good morning, Viewers! I said "viewers," didn't I? That's because today we are going to talk about things that we need to pay attention to as we are viewing visual images. Graphic designers, artists, and photographers all use various techniques to focus the viewer's attention on particular objects and people in their images. We call this *signifying* things. That means that artists are suggesting that certain objects and people are more significant and the viewer should pay special attention to them. So, before we can interpret any images, we have to figure out what the artist or photographer is trying to get the viewer to look at.

There are three common ways that artists or illustrators signify elements in their images or illustrations. One way is by making the object bigger or putting it in the front of the image. We call this *foregrounding*. If you look at any of the first few pages in Allen Say's book *Grandfather's Journey* (1993), it's pretty obvious that you are supposed to look first at the people in these portraits. They are the biggest element in the illustrations and dominate the page.

A second way that illustrators call the viewer's attention to things is through focusing. Have you ever taken a photograph of someone up close and then when you looked at it, everything else around the person is blurry or out of focus? Well, that's technically called *depth of field*. Photographers use this technique to point your attention to the objects in focus and not the blurry parts of the image. The larger the depth of field, the more a large part of the image is in focus. The smaller the depth of field, the smaller the section of the image is in focus.

A third way that illustrators call your attention to things is through color. Let's take a look at *Rose Blanche* by Roberto Innocenti (1985). In some of the illustrations, the color red is used to call your attention to the Nazi symbol and to Rose Blanche, the little girl in the red coat. When everything in the background of an illustration is one color and one element is a different color, it stands out and you seem to naturally look at to that part of the illustration. These are just three ways that illustrators call your attention to objects and people. We will surely discuss and explore more of them as we proceed through the year.

Instructional Trajectory: Understanding how illustrators signify various elements of their images is an important technique for viewers to develop. Artists want us to pay attention to certain things in order to understand what is important. As we are showing readers images, we want to ask them what catches their eye. What is it about this image that you first look at when we hold it up? Often our first perceptions of an image are important to better understand what the artist is trying to say to the viewer or reader.

Classroom Artifacts: Creating a list of ways that illustrators signify importance makes a good reference chart for these lessons (see Figure 7.6).

Closing Comments: These artistic techniques are used to call the viewer's attention to various elements of a visual image. Viewers with this knowledge can consider why the artist is trying to call their attention to one aspect of an image and not another. There is no specific formula at work here, it is simply another tool for considering what the illustrator is doing with their illustrations.

FIG. 7.6 *Signifying Elements*

- color
- focus—depth of field
- foreground—background
- size
- contrast
- use of frames or borders
- pointed at—gesture
- looks out of place—anomalous
- lighting—spotlight on object

Image Zones

The Challenge: Where objects and people are placed in an image gives them more or less importance. Whether something is on the top or bottom, left side or right side, has an effect on how we interpret an image. These various *image zones* are often discounted when readers are examining an image. Too often, readers are concerned with what is in the image and not where the contents are located.

Our Intentions: Drawing on the work of Gunther Kress and Theo van Leeuwen (1996), we will introduce readers to three primary image zones and explain how these zones contribute to the potential meanings of a visual image.

Lesson Overview: Utilizing the illustrations in the picturebooks of Anthony Browne, we will examine image zones used in various visual designs and how these zones add to the potential meanings of an image or illustration.

Language of Instruction: Good morning, Viewers! Today we are going to examine some images from some of the Anthony Browne picturebooks we have read this year—but we are going to look at them in new ways. I have selected particular illustrations from some of Browne's work for us to consider. First, I want to introduce you to the concept of *image zones*. There are three primary image zones or visual relationships that we will discuss. They are: (1) top-bottom, (2) left-right, and (3) center-margin. When objects are placed on top of other objects we give them more attention and therefore they have more power in the image. Sometimes the objects or people on the top are what we would like to have or be (ideal) and the bottom half is what it takes to get there (real). Let's look at some images from *Piggybook* (1986) and *Voices in the Park* (2001). In one image in *Piggybook*, the mother is standing over the father and the two boys, all of whom have turned into pigs, looking down on them. This image suggests that at this point the mother has more power over the rest of the family. On the next page, we see the father and the two boys groveling and looking up at the viewer. They seem to be sorry for what they did and are willing to give up their power to the mother. This is the top-bottom relationship that I mentioned.

In *Voices in the Park*, there are several examples of left-right zones being used to provide information. In the image where the father and Smudge are heading to the park, we see images of the Mona Lisa and The Laughing Man crying as the father and Smudge walk past. The left zone suggests the old place, or past-time frame, from where they have been, and the right zone is the new or where they are headed. Another good example is in *The Tunnel* (1997). There is an image where the boy and girl are being sent off to play. There is a hand pointing to where they are headed on the left side and the end of a building on the right side. The left side is where they were, the old information, and the right side is where they are going, or the new information.

The third type of image zone is when an artist places an important object or person in the center of an image and uses the margins for supporting details. One example in *Voices in the Park* is during the Fourth Voice when Smudge is looking up at Charles' Mom. Her face is placed in the center with some details, like the dogs running and the fruit on her coat, all of which surround her face.

These are just a few examples we could look at. Now, I think you should explore some images yourselves. I have some more Anthony Browne books and some picturebooks by other illustrators so we can take a look at how they use these different image zones.

Instructional Trajectory: As readers become familiar with the concepts and vocabulary of visual images and design, they should begin to use these concepts to explore the images they encounter. Teachers will need to demonstrate these ideas into the future and support students utilizing these concepts when they are reading aloud or sharing images in small groups.

Classroom Artifacts: A chart listing the three primary images zones can be constructed.

Closing Comments: This lesson could focus on magazine advertisements, websites, or expository texts. The placement of objects in advertisements is very calculated and important to the message of the image. In fact, there are often better examples of these concepts in magazines and other advertisements than in picturebooks.

FIG. 7.7 *Image Zones*

- ❖ top—ideal
- ❖ bottom—real
- ❖ left—old information
- ❖ right—new information
- ❖ center—importance
- ❖ margins—supporting details

Modality

The Challenge: In children's literature, there exists a range of modalities from realistic images to images that are considered imaginary or less "real." *Modality* is a term that means the "reality value" in an image. When pigs are dressed as humans in cartoonlike drawings there is low modality. When illustrators use realistic photography in their texts, there is generally high modality. Readers need to understand the various ways that artists and graphic designers exhibit markers of reality and make-believe.

Our Intentions: This lesson will focus on several visual design elements and techniques used to produce credibility or high modality in illustrations and visual images. The concept of modality is a cue for helping readers understand how an image or a text is to be approached.

Lesson Overview: Drawing on visual images in fictional literature and expository texts, we will demonstrate the various techniques artists use to render high or low modality. We would expect more abstract, imaginary images in fiction and more realistic images in nonfiction, but this may not always be the case.

Language of Instruction: Good morning, Viewers! How do we know what is real and what is imaginary when we look at an illustration? [*Discussion*] OK, those are some interesting ideas. Let me share with you a few more ideas. Is a black-and-white picture of your house more real than a color drawing of the same house? Let's take a look at the chart I have created that lists some things that we need to consider when we are deciding whether an image is real or imaginary (see Figure 7.8). What we are talking about is called *modality*. This means the reality value of an image, or how real it is. Some images portray the real world, and some portray imaginary things. We can use these clues when we are trying to make sense of a story.

First, we can take a look at the color used in an image, or the absence of color, like in black-and-white images. It is suggested that black-and-white photographs are not as lifelike as color photography. The second idea is context. When we see an animal in its natural habitat, it is more real than when we see it on a plain color background. Third, we can look at whether the whole image is in focus, like we normally see the world, or whether one object is in focus and the rest is blurry. The fourth, and maybe the most important idea, is the level of abstraction. Abstraction means how "lifelike" an image appears. Does it look the way we normally see things or is it drawn like a stick figure? For example, in one of our favorite David Wiesner books, *The Three Pigs* (2001), we noticed how Wiesner drew the pigs more realistically when they came out of certain illustrations. That is an example of the differences in modality and how Wiesner used this concept to distinguish between two levels of his story. If we ask ourselves about these four ideas—color, context, focus, and abstraction—we can decide whether an artist wants us to believe the image is real or not. Let's take a look at some images in picturebooks and some expository texts to determine their modality or reality value.

Instructional Trajectory: This concept may seem like something that we do naturally and often take for granted. However, as we start looking at the modality of an image, we get a window into what the illustrator may be trying to do. Hopefully, students will continue to question the reality value of images as they encounter them in a variety of contexts.

Classroom Artifacts: A chart outlining the types of modality, probably best represented as a continuum from imaginary to realistic, would benefit students. Copies of images that demonstrate varying degrees of modality would be most appropriate.

Closing Comments: The primary way that artists, photographers, and graphic designers produce real or credible images is by having them closely relate to the world as we experience it. This is called *naturalism*. There is a close correspondence between the representation and the way we experience the object in our world. Because of this, photography seems to be the most realistic of all media, but it is not quite that simple. We can increase the contrast, color saturation, or brightness of an image until it no longer resembles what was captured on film. The way a photograph is rendered can alter its modality.

FIG. 7.8 *Examples of Modality Charts*

Color Values—black and white to full color

Context—objects in real situations to out of context

Focus—all in focus to shallow depth of field

Abstraction—cartoonlike to realistic photography

Perspective and Viewing Distance

The Challenge: When we view an image that includes people, the characters in the visual image may be presented facing the viewer, turning away from the viewer, close-up, or far away. The characters may also be even with our line of sight, above the viewer, or below the viewer. These various perspectives change the way we interpret the characters, the way we are being asked to relate to the characters, and the point of view to which we are given access.

Our Intentions: This lesson is designed to get readers to pay attention to how characters are positioned in the visual images in picturebooks, and what these various positions mean for interpreting the images.

Lesson Overview: Using a variety of texts by Chris Van Allsburg, Anthony Browne, and Colin Thompson, we will introduce readers to different perspectives in visual images and how these affect how we interpret the characters in visual images.

Language of Instruction: Good morning, Viewers! Today we are going to take a look at some of our favorite characters in picturebooks and discuss how these characters are presented to us in the images we encounter. Let's begin by examining whether the character we are considering is looking at us or looking at another character in the image. In *Voices in the Park* (Browne 2001), two of my favorite illustrations are the images in the Fourth Voice where Charles is sitting on the park bench with his mother and he is looking directly at us, and the image where he is leaving the park and he is looking back over his shoulder. When the character is looking directly at the viewer, he is asking us to pay attention to him. This is called a *demand*. We are being asked to attend to this character and interact with their situation. We have to ask why the character is looking at us and how we feel about the character.

When the character in an image is looking at another character or object, for example throughout the book *Looking for Atlantis* by Colin Thompson (1993), we are being "offered" a window into their world, sometimes through their perspective. In *Looking for Atlantis* the boy character never looks directly at the viewer. Instead we are asked to consider what he sees and the way he is trying to make sense of his world. These are two very different relationships between the character and the viewer.

The next thing we have to consider is whether the character is above our sight line, so we are looking up at them, below our sight line where we would look down at them, or lined up with us, looking straight at us. When we are looking up at someone, we seem to be in a position of less power. When we look down on a character, we are given a position of more power, and looking at a character evenly in the eye usually means we are equals. One good example is in the Fourth Voice in *Voices in the Park* where Smudge is looking up at the mother. The mother is peering down at her and seems to be upset. By positioning her above the viewer, we are placed in a position of less power and the character is given more power over us.

The last thing I want to call your attention to is whether the characters are close-up or far away in the image. In faraway or scenic shots, we get more context. Like in *Jumanji* by Chris Van Allsburg (1981), there are some images where the viewer is placed way above and far away from the characters and setting. When Van Allsburg does that, we are more detached from the characters and get a sense of where they live and where they are going. In some images in *Jumanji*, we are very close to the characters and animals in the story. We get a close-up view and are more intimately involved in the action. By changing the perspectives, distances, and which direction the character faces, we are being asked to relate to the characters in different ways. We need to pay attention to how illustrators position various objects and characters to better interpret their images.

Instructional Trajectory: It is important for readers to begin paying attention to issues of power between characters and between the image and the viewer. How characters are positioned determines the relationship we construct with them and how we understand the illustrations.

Classroom Artifacts: A chart could be prepared with several questions to get students to pay attention to the perspectives being offered in the images of a picturebook (see Figure 7.9).

FIG. 7.9 *Questions Regarding Perspective*

Look at an image or illustration and ask yourself the following questions:

1. Do any of the characters look directly at the viewer? When do they do this, and why are they doing it?

2. Are the characters close-up or far away in the images? Does this change throughout the story? What might this mean?

3. Are there times when we are above, below, or equal with the characters' line of sight? What might the artist be trying to do with these positions?

4. When the character looks directly at us, do we feel sorry for them, or do we understand what they are going through?

Closing Comments: Perspective is an important consideration in viewing a piece of art but one that is rarely discussed. It seems natural to us to look at an image and have the character stare back at us like the Mona Lisa. However, when the character is placed in different positions, above or below the viewer, the perspective changes and so does our relationship to the characters. There are numerous examples within picturebooks of these techniques being employed. As teachers, we need to begin paying closer attention to how things are included in images, not simply what is included.

Artistic Styles

The Challenge: All artistic techniques are not the same, nor do they convey the same message. As Marshall McLuhan stated, "the medium is the message." In order to fully comprehend what is included in an image, we have to consider how the message is presented to us. Novice readers have little experience with a variety of artistic styles and movements, but even a cursory discussion can awaken readers to the variety of media that they have encountered numerous times in picturebooks.

Our Intentions: This lesson is designed as an introduction to artistic styles and how they affect our interpretations of images. We have selected four artistic styles from among the many styles available to discuss and will present each with examples from children's literature illustrations.

Lesson Overview: Drawing on a variety of picturebooks, we will demonstrate various illustration styles and how they affect our understandings of a visual image.

Language of Instruction: Good morning, Artists! That's right, I said artists again. Today we are going to talk about different types of art and how they have affected picturebook illustrations. For each artistic style, I have found an example in some of the books we have read so far this year. Let me begin by giving you the names of the styles or artistic movements (see Figure 7.10). Each of these styles uses different media and offers different possibilities when we try to interpret them.

Let's begin with *realism*. Realism means the artist tries to paint or draw images that are closely related to the way the world looks to us. Paul Zelinsky's *Rapunzel* (1997) is an example of realism. He has tried to paint the people as they look to him, paying close attention to details and the setting. Another example is *Saint George and the Dragon*, illustrated by Trina Schart Hyman (Hodges 1984). She uses detailed, lifelike illustrations to represent the events in the story. In these illustrations, we are asked to see the people and scenes as portrayals of the way things really are.

Impressionism is a movement that began as a reaction to realism, or the realist style. Impressionist painters wanted to depict the changing light and colors of objects because they changed as time and perspective changed. One of the most famous impressionist painters, Claude Monet, used to paint numerous images of his garden and lily pond. The images painted by Emily Arnold McCully in *Mirette on the High Wire* (1992), which took place in France close to where Monet painted, are considered impressionist style.

Notice how the paintings seem blurry or not quite as precise and detailed as the realist style. Maurice Sendak uses an impressionist style in *Mr. Rabbit and the Lovely Present* written by Charlotte Zolotow (1962). His outdoor scenes in this picturebook remind me of some of the impressionist art I have seen in museums. Impressionist illustrations portray the world as it is seen from different perspectives and times.

One of the artistic styles we have seen lately is called *surrealism*. This style is usually associated with the work of Rene Magritte and Salvador Dali, two very famous artists. Surrealist painters combine things in surprising ways to get the viewer to reconsider what they are looking at. Their images are sometimes puzzling and confusing, but usually funny and interesting to look at. Two illustrators we have experienced that draw on surrealism are Colin Thompson and, of course, Anthony Browne. In his picturebooks, like *Changes* (1990) and *Voices in the Park* (2001), Anthony Browne puts things together in strange ways and adds details to his images we sometimes don't expect. The same with Colin Thompson. In *Looking for Atlantis* (1993) and *The Paradise Garden* (1988), Thompson adds some strange and unexpected items to his backgrounds. One thing for sure, the illustrations of both of these artists require us to slow down and spend some time looking at the details of their images. By putting together two objects that we wouldn't normally associate with each other, we are invited to reconsider each of the objects and their relationship with one another.

The last type of artistic style I am going to share with you today is called *folk art*. Folk art is an artistic style that was developed by craftsmen and what are sometimes called "local artists." Some folk art includes quilts, tole painting, embroidery, and woodworking. Two good examples of illustrators that draw on folk art techniques are Faith Ringgold in her book *Tar Beach* (1991), and Simms Taback in his book *Joseph Had a Little Overcoat* (1999). In both of these books, quilts and fabrics are used throughout the illustrations. Folk art is designed to make people feel comfortable, to recognize things from their own lives, and to be able to relate to these pieces of art.

There are many more art styles, and as the year goes on we will look into some of them. The important thing is not to be able to label the artistic style as much as it is important to understand what artists are trying to make us think about and feel when we see their art.

Instructional Trajectory: It is our hope that the discussions of artistic style will carry over into art class, any field trips to art museums, and looking at images in picturebooks and other settings. Understanding artistic style is simply another way of analyzing visual images to consider what the illustrator is trying to do.

Classroom Artifacts: Create a chart with each artistic style and some images that represent that style. Providing examples from art and from picturebook art would be helpful.

FIG. 7.10 *Artistic Styles*

❖   Realism

❖   Impressionism

❖   Surrealism

❖   Folk Art

Closing Comments: There are numerous references that help expand one's understandings of art and artistic styles in picturebooks. Some of our favorites are:

Doonan, Jane. 1993. *Looking at Pictures in Picture Books*. Stroud, UK: Thimble Press.

Evans, Janet. 1998. *What's in the Picture? Responding to Illustrations in Picture Books*. London, UK: Paul Chapman.

Kiefer, Barbara Z. 1995. *The Potential of Picturebooks: From Visual Lliteracy to Aesthetic Understanding*. Englewood Cliffs, NJ: Prentice-Hall.

Lewis, David. 2001. *Reading Contemporary Picturebooks: Picturing Text*. London, UK: Routledge Falmer.

Nikolajeva, Maria, and Carole Scott. 2006. *How Picturebooks Work*. New York: Routledge.

Nodelman, Perry. 1984. "How Picture Books Work." In *Image and Maker: An Annual Dedication to the Consideration of Book Illustration*, edited by H. Darling and P. Neumeyer. La Jolla, CA: Green Tiger Press.

Stewig, John Warren. 1995. *Looking at Picture Books*. Fort Atkinson, WI: Highsmith Press.

Interpreting Texts Through Literary Theories

Teaching complex literary theories to young readers seems a fool's errand to many teachers. And yet unless we present the theoretical lenses we draw upon to interpret literature, we often mask the ideologies and criteria we use to warrant particular interpretations over others. There are no neutral interpretations of texts. As readers, we draw upon the resources, values, and interpretive repertoires available to make sense of the texts we encounter. Books don't read themselves, and we each bring a particular perspective to the texts we read, whether we realize what these are or not.

The lessons in this section are designed to call students' attention to the various theoretical lenses available to us as readers. Although many of these literary theories can be complex and seem inaccessible to young readers, it does not mean there aren't ways of introducing them to the readers in our classrooms. Throughout this series of lessons, we have tried to present various literary theories without losing their original intent. In other words, we don't want to "dumb down" the content of the various theoretical lenses we present, just simplify the means we use to present these concepts and the language we use in our instructional practices.

As educators, we often find ourselves reading pedagogical publications or how-to books about teaching. We feel it is important to balance our reading of books about pedagogy with our reading in literary and other theories. It may be all right for our intermediate students not to completely understand these theories, but teachers should become well-versed with their foundations and their uses in interpreting classic and contemporary literature. Reading outside of the field of education, and going beyond the volume of pedagogical materials presented in university course work and inservice workshops, is a valuable strategy for classroom teachers, one that we endorse quite enthusiastically.

Three books that have been extremely helpful in conceptualizing our own lessons in comprehension and to our understandings of literary theories are:

Appleman, D. 2000. *Critical Encounters in High School English: Teaching Literary Theory to Adolescents.* New York: Teachers College Press.

Eckert, L. S. 2006. *How Does It Mean?: Engaging Reluctant Readers Through Literary Theory.* Portsmouth, NH: Heinemann.

Noell Moore, J. 1997. *Interpreting Young Adult Literature: Literary Theory in the Secondary Classroom.* Portsmouth, NH: Boynton/Cook.

The comprehension lessons in this section include:

Archetypes in Literature

The Challenge: Finding symbols in literature and poetry has been challenging students for what seems like forever. Personally, we spent many years in classrooms poring over texts to locate the symbols we knew that our teacher would point out to us in the next day's class discussion. Northrop Frye (1957), drawing on the work of Carl Jung, created a typology of archetypes, or common patterns, for characters, themes, and events in literature. We will use his typology to help readers recognize various common symbols and archetypes in both classic and contemporary literature.

Our Intentions: We will introduce some of the most common archetypes to our readers to help them see the commonalities across works of literature, and be better able to draw personal connections to these texts. Although we won't be going into as much depth with this concept as we would with college or high school students, we want to present this material without dumbing it down for our students.

Lesson Overview: In this lesson, we will present several of the most common archetypes, including the heroic quest, the trickster, death and rebirth, protagonist and antagonist, journey, earth mother, and creation. Drawing on the novels we have read, we will use Natalie Babbit's *Tuck Everlasting* (1975) as our cornerstone text to introduce most of these archetypes.

Language of Instruction: Good morning, Readers! This morning we are going to venture into new territories. Has anyone ever heard of the word *archetypes*? Well, this may be a new term for many of you. What it means is a common pattern or theme that has been used in literature for literally centuries. Some of the most common archetypes are listed on the chart behind me. Many of these came from one person's study of mythology and literature. His name was Northrop Frye (1957). He discovered that many classic texts drew on the same themes and patterns to get readers to react to texts in particular ways. What we are going to do today is think about the novel *Tuck Everlasting*, and see if we recognize any of Northrop Frye's archetypes in this story. For example, one of the archetypes Frye mentions is that of the journey or quest. In *Tuck Everlasting*, Winnie Foster is on a journey to find the Tuck family and the magic spring. We have to ask ourselves, "What does a journey do for us?" [*Discussion*] A journey is a search or a quest for things outside of ourselves. A quest is usually conceived as a process, as an adventure where one learns new things as they travel along. Let's consider what Winnie may have learned on her adventure. Let's talk about this, then we can look at other archetypes on our list.

Instructional Trajectory: The goal in these lessons is not to be able to simply identify each and every archetype, but to become aware that archetypes are frequently used by authors to construct stories or retell myths. We want readers to use their knowledge of these archetypes to recognize common patterns in the new texts they encounter, how the author might use them to tell their story, and to draw upon them to make sense of what they are reading.

Classroom Artifacts: Teachers can prepare a class chart listing Frye's archetypes and some brief descriptions of each one. This chart can be extended to include examples of various archetypes and how they might add to the meaning of a particular story (see Figure 8.1).

Closing Comments: This is certainly an introductory treatment of a much deeper concept, but one that may help call readers' awareness to interesting patterns and themes. It is just possible that the reason we struggled to find symbols in books is because we didn't know what the possibilities were. Northrop Frye's work helps us to recognize those patterns and possibilities in literature.

FIG. 8.1 *Common Archetypes*

The Archetype	The Text	Example	What It Does for the Story or Reader?
The Hero			
The Quest			
Death and Rebirth			
The Trickster			
Protagonist			
Antagonist			
Earth Mother			

Historical Criticism

The Challenge: In all too many classrooms, books are read to students without reference to the author, illustrator, or time period in which the text was constructed. Teachers simply pick up a book, mention the title, and start reading from the opening page of the story. We have discussed how to approach a fictional text (see Lesson 2.1), so we will try to expand on that concept here. For this lesson, the focus is on helping readers understand the history of a work, and how authors' experiences and backgrounds affect their writing.

Our Intentions: This lesson will draw on several texts and some biographical information pertaining to the author and illustrator to help students consider historical or autobiographical perspectives for interpreting a text.

Lesson Overview: Using *Where the Wild Things Are* by Maurice Sendak as a point of reference, we will focus on a variety of epitextual resources, including biographical information, author and illustrator interviews, and critical analyses to explore new possibilities for interpreting this classic picturebook.

Language of Instruction: Good morning, Readers! Today, we are going to go back and talk about one of my, and I hope it's one of your, favorite picturebooks, *Where the Wild Things Are* by Maurice Sendak (1963). Instead of focusing on the book itself this time, we are going to focus on the time period in which the book was written, some critical analyses written by a variety literary critics, and the actual life and experiences of Maurice Sendak. Let's begin with an interview I found on the Internet where Sendak explains that the book was originally going to be called *Where the Wild Horses Are*. Isn't that interesting? [*Discussion*] In the interview Sendak says he could not draw horses very well, so he changed the characters from horses into "wild things." I'm glad he did! In another interview, Sendak explained that he was a sickly child and that when he played in the yard his mother would watch over him out the back window of their house. In this section of the interview, he says that he put the moon in Max's bedroom window to represent his mother watching over him. We talked a great deal about the moon, but we never discussed his mother. If we didn't look outside the book, or at epitextual resources we would never know what he was thinking. Let's look at some more information I found out about Maurice Sendak. Did you know that *Where the Wild Things Are* is actually the first book in a trilogy that contains *In the Night Kitchen* (1970) and *Outside, Over There* (1981)? We could certainly talk about how these three books are related. We could also read some analyses written by literary critics to see how they came to understand this book. All of these resources outside of the book influence how we interpret a book, and we need to be sure we consider them as we negotiate our understandings of this classic picturebook.

Instructional Trajectory: As teachers, when we present a book for reading aloud, we need to be sure to attend to the author and publication date, discussing what we know about authors and illustrators that may influence our interpretations. In reader-response notebooks, we may begin to ask students to consider an author's purpose and background in their entries.

Classroom Artifacts: A class chart focusing on elements of a particular author's or illustrator's life may be supportive of our discussions. We would suggest collecting epitextual resources—critical analyses, interviews, author and illustrator biographies, advertisements, and other information focusing on particular books we may revisit throughout our lessons.

Closing Comments: *Where the Wild Things Are* is one of the most frequently analyzed and discussed picturebooks of all time. A quick perusal of the Internet or library resources reveals numerous entries and biographical information. We have been collecting information about children's authors and illustrators for years, and we make this information available in our classrooms. Knowing about the background of an author or the time period a book was created in can extend discussions and help readers construct new and more sophisticated interpretations.

Narrative Analysis

The Challenge: When people tell stories or *oral narratives*, there is an underlying structure to the way these stories are created. Knowing the elements of oral narratives helps readers understand how written stories are structured and the various elements of that structure. There are similarities and difference between the stories told through oral language and those relayed through written language. Knowing more about *book language* will help readers become better at comprehending written narratives.

Our Intentions: Using William Labov and Joshua Waletzky's work (1967) on the analysis of oral narratives and the various structures they researched and created, we will analyze a few fictional stories to understand how they are structured and use this analysis to help readers better comprehend written narratives.

Lesson Overview: Using a story the class is familiar with, in this case several versions of the fairy tale of the three pigs, we will discuss Labov and Waletzky's narrative structures and how they help readers comprehend fictional narratives.

Language of Instruction: Good morning, Readers! In today's lesson, we are going to look at an old fairy tale, the story of the three pigs, from a new perspective. The perspective is called *narrative analysis*. Literary theorists have done research on how people tell stories and have analyzed these stories to find their underlying structures. I thought that by sharing some of these underlying structures with you, we would be able to comprehend the stories we hear and read even better. Let's take a look at the chart behind me (see Figure 8.2). There are sometimes five or six elements in a story depending on how it is told. What I thought we would do is use the picturebook *The Three Little Pigs* by Steven Kellogg (1997) to demonstrate how these structures are involved in the stories we tell and read.

The first element is called the *orientation*. In the orientation, we are introduced to the characters, setting, and situation of the story. Can anyone tell me what the orientation to the three little pigs story is? [*Discussion*] OK, now the second element is called the *complicating action*. In *The Three Little Pigs*, the complicating action is when the mother pig sends her three sons out to seek their fortune. The wolf realizes the pigs are out in the world and figures he can capture an easy meal. By sending the three pigs out into the world, the narrator is setting them up for the challenges they will face. The next element is called the *results*. In this element, we learn how the three pigs solve or don't solve the problem we learned about in the complicating action. The first two pigs solved their problems by running to the third pig's house, and the third pig solved the problem by building his house out of bricks.

The next element is called the *evaluation*, and it is a bit trickier. In the story of the three little pigs, we are led to believe that the third pig is smarter and that by doing his work, and not playing around, he will be better off. The evaluation is like the point or purpose of the story. It seems the point of this story is to listen to your mother and do your work the best you can.

After the evaluation, there is some type of resolution to the story. The story is drawn to a close and many of our questions are answered and problems are resolved. The last element is called the *coda*. The coda in a narrative is like a coda in music: the ending returns to and relates back to the beginning. Some stories have them, and some stories don't. There isn't a coda with this story, but if there were it might focus on how the three pigs returned to their mother and told her about their experiences. Let's take a look at some of the other fairy tales we know and using these narrative elements try to better understand these familiar stories.

Instructional Trajectory: The narrative analysis we have undertaken should reveal patterns in most of the written narratives we encounter. By calling attention to these elements and structures during subsequent discussions and during the reading aloud of various chapter books, we can enhance our students' interpretive repertoires. Also, we would expect to see evidence of this type of analysis in our students' reader-response notebooks.

Classroom Artifacts: A class chart outlining the elements of narrative should be displayed (see Figure 8.2).

Closing Comments: Although Labov and Waletzky's research was done primarily on oral narratives, it is an effective device for analyzing written narratives as well. Once again, the goal is not to simply discover or name the various elements, but to understand how it affects the stories we read.

FIG. 8.2 *Elements of Narrative*

❖ Orientation—the orientation introduces the reader to the persons, places, time and behavioral situation.

❖ Complicating Action—the complicating action describes the challenge or conflict that the characters face and must deal with throughout the story.

❖ Result—the complicating action ends in a result, where conflict ends or problems are resolved.

❖ Evaluation—the evaluation is a judgment or the intended significance of the events recounted in the previous sections. It helps the reader understand the point or the purpose of the story.

❖ Resolution—the resolution follows the evaluation; it draws the story to a close.

❖ Coda—in some stories, but not all, the author will include a reference back to the orientation and complicating action that brings the reader full circle in the story.

Symbolic Interpretations

The Challenge: Authors and illustrators use written and visual symbols to make connections between what is written and represented and what is meant. Too often, we focus on the symbols that students miss and not the ones that affect their reading. In other words, it's the symbols we recognize that have the greatest impact on our interpretations, not the ones we miss. Whether blatantly obvious or obscure, symbols make connections across texts, personal experiences, and the meanings we construct.

Our Intentions: This lesson will discuss some of the most common verbal and visual symbols used by authors and illustrators, and ask students to inquire into the texts they read to find other examples of symbolic representations.

Lesson Overview: Beginning with common everyday symbols, and using the book *Martin's Big Words* by Doreen Rappaport (2001), we will spend time constructing our own understandings of symbolic representations and how they affect our understandings of the books we read.

Language of Instruction: Good morning, Readers! Does anyone know what this means? [*Hold up a red circle and slash with a cigarette inside the circle.*] That's right, it means "no" depending on what is included inside the circle. For example, this symbol means no smoking. These symbols are immediately recognized by most people because they are used everywhere. In other words, people all agree on what they mean. Other examples could be a stop sign, or the boy and girl symbols on some bathroom doors. We know what these symbols mean because over time we have learned what they mean.

Authors and illustrators use symbols in their writing and images to mean things as well. Some of them are pretty straightforward, while others may not be immediately understandable. Some of the literary symbols that we might immediately recognize are: a rose for love, the color black for death, a green tree for life or rebirth, or a pitchfork for the devil. Well, today we are going to read *Martin's Big Words* by Doreen Rappaport, illustrated by Bryan Collier. In the back of the book Bryan Collier has described many of the symbols he included in the illustrations and what he meant by each of them. However, before we look in the back of the book to see what Collier wrote about his illustrations and the symbols he included, we are going to read the book and look at the illustrations to see what meanings we get from the text and images.

Instructional Trajectory: Searching for symbols is a never-ending process of drawing connections between the way things are represented in images and words, and the meanings we attribute to these symbols.

Classroom Artifacts: A chart depicting some universal symbols and some literary symbols might be beneficial. Many of the symbolic relationships can be understood by reading interviews with authors and illustrators. Some symbols are universal, while others are specific to a particular book or culture.

Closing Comments: We need to be careful that we don't reduce the reading of literature or the viewing of images to a search for symbols. When students learn that they continually miss all the important symbols, they often stop worrying about making sense of the text and end up on a symbol scavenger hunt. We don't want our search for symbols to end up like the traditional search for the hidden main idea. Symbols influence our reading when we make the connection between representation and meaning, not when we miss them.

Reader-Response Criticism

The Challenge: Readers often talk about how a book made them feel, and teachers often ask about these affective responses to texts, but rarely do they inquire into *why* they responded they way they did. Reader-response criticism *begins* with readers' responses to literature, including aesthetic response, but uses these responses as the starting point for analysis of a text or an image.

Our Intentions: The literary critic Wolfgang Iser (1978) discussed the concept of *gap-filling* by readers of fictional texts. What he meant by this was that all written text was partial, that language was incapable of carrying complete meanings, and that readers in their transactions with texts filled in the gaps from their own experiences and understandings. This lesson is designed to get readers to consider the reasons they respond to texts the way they do. In other words, readers fill these literary gaps in different ways, and how they are filled in is an important aspect in understanding one's response to a text.

Lesson Overview: Beginning with simpler picturebooks, like *Rosie's Walk* by Pat Hutchins (1968), and *Lily Takes a Walk* by Satoshi Kitamura (1998), we will demonstrate how one's personal and cultural experiences help readers fill in the gaps in stories. During these lessons, the texts we use will get more complex, and will require readers to reflect on the experiences and understandings drawn upon to fill in gaps in the text, and thus comprehend what we read.

Language of Instruction: Good morning, Readers! Today, we are going to begin by taking a look at some picturebooks that at first glance look rather simple. But don't be fooled, these short texts actually require some sophisticated interpretations in order to understand what is happening. The first picturebook is called *Rosie's Walk* by Pat Hutchins. [*Briefly read and discuss book*.] As we went through the story we had to infer what was happening to the fox and how that related to what Rosie did. In this next book, *Lily Takes a Walk* by Satoshi Kitamura, we will have to do some additional inferring to understand what is happening. [*Briefly read and discuss book*.] The things we inferred were affected by the experiences we have had in our lives. If we worked on a farm, or if we lived in a city, it would affect how we read these books.

There are things left out of every book we read. It's not the fault of the author or illustrator, it is simply impossible to include everything in the text and images. What we need to do is to begin to pay attention to how we fill in gaps in a text and what experiences and knowledge we use to do so. Now let's take a look at a more complex picturebook, and eventually we will talk about this idea of gap-filling with a short novel. We are going to read *Wolves* by Emily Gravett (2006). [*Read and discuss book.*] There are lots of things left out of this story, aren't there? Let's discuss some of the things that we brought to this picturebook from our experiences with other texts and our lives. For example, our knowledge of fairy tales may have influenced our understandings. Also, if we know a lot about wolves that would affect our interpretations. Once we start analyzing what we bring to a text, we can begin to understand ourselves as readers, and why our interpretations differ from other readers' interpretations.

Instructional Trajectory: Keeping in mind that comprehending a text involves filling in gaps, inferring, and connecting to one's experiences means that the way students respond during discussions and in writing may take on a more insightful, or even aesthetic, slant. We need to listen closely to the ways that students respond to texts, and help them inquire into why they responded the way they do. Calling one's perspective and background into focus leads to more conscious, deliberate reading.

Classroom Artifacts: A variety of charts describing how readers fill gaps might be appropriate, although much of this may remain at the verbal and cognitive levels. Any chart that focuses on this concept must remain open for a variety of interpretations and avoid the temptation to strive for consensus.

Closing Comments: Understanding why we respond to texts the way we do can have a profound influence on our reading identities. Through these lessons, we come to each subsequent text more open to investigating why we like, dislike, connect, stay away from, and react to the texts of our lives. In the classroom, this means a deeper level of discussion and a more introspective stance toward reading.

Feminist Perspectives on Literature

The Challenge: Feminist literary theory focuses on the portrayal of women in literature, their absence from stories, and the patriarchal systems that serve to marginalize women in society. Often considered too advanced a concept for novice readers, the portrayal of gender is an important concept to discuss in the elementary and middle grades. Traditionally, women and girls have been depicted in subservient roles in children's literature. We cannot wait until high school to discuss these issues.

Our Intentions: Being able to disrupt commonplace assumptions of the roles that women and men adopt in literature is the starting point for critiquing literature from a feminist or gender perspective. Beginning with more obvious examples of female and male characters and progressing to more subtle forms of gender bias is the focus of this lesson.

Lesson Overview: This lesson will begin with understanding how men and women are often portrayed in literature and some ideas for "reading against" these portrayals. Using fairy tales, contemporary picturebooks, and some classic novels, this series of lessons is designed to help readers analyze and discuss traditional and contemporary gender roles and expectations.

Language of Instruction: Good morning, Ladies and Gentlemen! Have you ever noticed how we often divide ourselves along gender lines? By gender lines, I mean how we divide the world into men and women, boys and girls. In literature, we can look at how women and men are portrayed when they are included in a story, and what they are expected to do or become. In order to do this, we are going to begin with two books, *Piggybook* by Anthony Browne (1986), and *Horace and Morris But Mostly Dolores* by James Howe (1999). Before we read and discuss these stories, let me ask you these two questions, "What are the best and worst things about being a boy or a girl?" and "How would your lives be different if you were the opposite gender?" [*Discuss answers and create chart.*] OK, now let's read these two books with our answers to these questions in mind. [*Read and discuss books.*] We are going to create a *character timeline* for each of these two books. What we will do is draw a straight line to represent the duration of one of the stories and then fill in points along the line to describe how the character evolved through the story. Let me demonstrate this idea by creating a character timeline for the Mom in *Piggybook* (see Figure 8.3).

| Mom does the work at home. | Mom is treated poorly. | Mom doesn't come home. | The boys and Dad are sorry. |

FIG. 8.3 *Character Timeline Example*

Instructional Trajectory: This lesson is actually the opening lesson in a unit of study focusing on gender and gender portrayals in literature. Changing the way we think about gender, who can do what, who is supposed to act in what way, may be a difficult subject at times to address but essential if we are going to break some of the hegemonic systems of repression that occur along gender lines in our society.

Classroom Artifacts: Creating a list of students' responses to questions about gender and roles in society as well as their own character timelines would be beneficial. We have also included a list of questions for addressing gender issues in literature (see Figure 8.4).

Closing Comments: The example in Figure 8.3 is only an outline of the details that we could fill in for the characters we will discuss. The focus is on understanding how the character changes and the reasons for the change. These reasons can spur interesting discussions in intermediate and middle grade classrooms. It is during these years that young men and women are struggling with the onset of puberty and the roles they are expected to play in our society as gendered beings. Although there are times when these discussions may be uncomfortable, they are important topics to be discussed.

FIG. 8.4 *Additional Questions for Discussion*

How are boys and girls, or men and women portrayed?

Who seems to be absent from the stories?

Who is in charge or has the power in the story, men or women?

Do these characters' roles fit with your expectations for your gender?

Is the world portrayed in the book similar to the world you live in?

Issues of Power

The Challenge: In literature, as in life, certain people are given more power over other people. This power may come from their social status, occupation, family history, culture, ethnic background, nationality, gender, personality, education, or the amount of wealth they have accumulated. How power is dealt with in literature can reflect or challenge the systems of power in society. These issues of power often go unnoticed in our readings and discussions. Calling readers' attention to issues of power may help them confront inequities and challenge the systems that marginalize certain groups of people or individuals.

Our Intentions: Drawing upon Karl Marx's concepts of power and class struggle, this lesson serves as an introduction into looking closely at how issues of power are often masked by dominant ideologies in traditional and contemporary literature. Understanding who has the power in a story, and how that power is generated, exposes interesting ideas that can jump-start discussions.

Lesson Overview: Utilizing two of our favorite books by John Burningham, *Come Away from the Water, Shirley* (1977), and *Time to Get Out of the Bath, Shirley* (1978), we begin our discussion of issues of power by focusing on the relationship between parents and their children. In these two delightful, yet richly conceived picturebooks, Burningham offers Shirley a means of escaping the domination of her parents by using her imagination to create new and better worlds to explore. We have found this a common theme in much of children's literature.

Language of Instruction: Good morning, Readers! Today we are going to begin talking about power. What I mean by *power* is who gets to boss who around in a story. We are going to begin by reading two books by John Burningham, one of our favorite authors. The two books, *Come Away from the Water, Shirley*, and *Time to Get Out of the Bath, Shirley*, tell the story of a young girl named Shirley who does not like to be told what to do and has a rather large imagination. This sounds like many of you, doesn't it? Maybe you'll be able to relate to Shirley's plight in these stories. [*Read one or both books.*] Let's talk about Shirley and how she responds to her parents. Why is it that the parents in both books are able to tell Shirley what she has to do? Where does their power come from? We can take this discussion a step further and ask where your parents get the power to make you do things. Let's create a chart about where people get power and how this affects the meanings we construct in our experiences with texts.

Instructional Trajectory: As we mentioned in the opening sections, this lesson serves as an introduction to issues of power in literature. Taking the list that was created from the discussions surrounding Burningham's Shirley books, we can look at other characters in literature and discuss where they get their power from and whether we think this is equitable. Ideologies run deep, and our belief systems make many things appear natural, when in fact they are socially constructed. By attempting to "unpack" some of the things we think are natural or "just the way things are" we can begin to read against these issues presented in stories, and offer alternative interpretations that disrupt our commonplace assumptions.

Classroom Artifacts: Creating a chart of students' comments from the Shirley books serves as a guide for uncovering issues of power in other texts. In addition, having a list of "critical questions" to ask of subsequent books can call attention to ideologies and issues of power as we read forward (see Figure 8.5).

Closing Comments: Though I would not go in depth into reading the work of Karl Marx in the intermediate grades, using his ideas to explore issues of power is an exciting starting point for teachers' inquiries. Every text positions someone in authority and someone else in submission, and reveals the author's and society's ideologies toward certain people and the world. By discussing these issues of power, we are calling students' attention to the challenges they face and the constraints that may affect their futures.

FIG. 8.5 *Critical Questions for Issues of Power*

Who seems to have the power in this story?

Where did this power come from?

Who is marginalized or has little power in the story?

How are the marginalized characters "kept in their place"?

How do these issues relate to your own experiences?

Was there a shift in power during the story?

What caused the shift in power?

Psychoanalytical Perspectives

The Challenge: From a psychoanalytical perspective, one's interpretations are directly connected to one's identity, or as Norman Holland (1975) has defined it, one's *identity theme*. Readers draw upon their identity theme to bring certain features of a text to the forefront, and to allow others to retreat into the background. Readers use a piece of literature to symbolize their own fears, desires, and what they deem to have moral, intellectual, and social significance. This is challenging theoretical terrain, but we believe that teachers can draw upon Holland's concept of identity theme to support readers' interpretations of texts as a window into their psyches and identities.

Our Intentions: Beginning with some picturebooks that we have read and discussed previously, we will focus our students' attention on aspects of the stories that call forth things we desire, fear, and cause us to ponder. In order to consider these ideas we will need to move to a second level, studying the nature of our responses. Analyzing one's initial responses to a text is designed to help readers understand *why* they respond the way they do and what this says about their own lives and experiences.

Lesson Overview: This lesson focuses on a Reflecting on Our Responses project, which contains two parts. The first part entails reflecting on one's reading selections by creating a Personal Bookshelf. This is simply a list or collection of one's recent reading selections and one's favorite and most influential books. The second part is an analysis of one's reader-response notebook. Through this second part of the project, we are trying to get readers to interrogate why they respond to books the way they do, and come to understand what this reveals about their personality, values, fears, and desires.

Language of Instruction: Good morning, Readers! So far this year we have spent a lot of time responding to literature and other texts in a variety of formats and modes of expression. We have drawn pictures, acted out parts of books, written in our response notebooks, and discussed books as a whole class and in small groups. What we are going to do this week is reflect on our responses to literature and create a Reflecting on Our Responses project. This project will have two parts. The first part will entail creating a collection and inventory of our favorite books and those that have had the biggest impact on us, and the second part will be analyzing as many responses to these texts as we have available.

Let's begin by discussing some of the favorite books we have read as a class and then you can collect some of your personal favorites in your own Personal Bookshelf. [*Discuss books read.*] The books we have just mentioned may or may not have been some of your personal favorites. I would like you to begin by analyzing your reading logs and response notebooks and make a list of your favorites. Please be sure to list a variety of genres and texts so we can get a big picture of your reading.

After we do this we are going to conduct an analysis of our reader-response notebooks. I want you to go through your notebook and look for things that seem to be repeated— you know, some patterns in what you write about. Then I want you to also consider things we have talked about as a whole group, things like symbols, themes, mood, story structures, that you don't seem to be writing about. We are looking for patterns in what we do write about literature, and things we have seemed to overlook.

Instructional Trajectory: Coming to know oneself as a reader can reveal insights into ourselves as human beings. We reflect on our thinking in many situations, but school is the one place where we should be expected to do this on a regular basis. Unfortunately, this is not always the case. Too often after a response is generated to a story, the task is considered complete and students simply move on to the next story. Thinking about our thinking should have an effect on all aspects of the curriculum.

Classroom Artifacts: Each reader will create a Reflections on Our Responses project that is designed to get readers to better understand why they select certain texts, and why they respond to these texts the way they do.

Closing Comments: There is an old saying that goes, "If you are a hammer, everything you see looks like a nail." It applies to this version of reader-response theory. Our identities call particular aspects of literature to attention, and bypass other aspects. We need to reflect on the types of responses we generate when reading, allowing these responses to serve as a window into our own personalities.

Professional References

Alexander, Robin. 2006. *Toward Dialogic Teaching: Rethinking Classroom Talk*. 3d ed. Cambridge, UK: Dialogos.

Appleman, Deborah. 2000. *Critical Encounters in High School English: Teaching Literary Theory to Adolescents*. New York: Teachers College Press.

Arnheim, Rudolf. 1986. *Art and Visual Perception: A Psychology of the Creative Eye*. Berkeley: University of California Press.

Cazden, Courtney B. 2001. *Classroom Discourse: The Language of Teaching and Learning*. 2d ed. Portsmouth, NH: Heinemann.

Chambers, Aidan. 1996. *Tell Me: Children, Reading, and Talk*. York, ME: Stenhouse.

Culler, Jonathan. 1997. *Literary Theory: A Very Short Introduction*. Oxford, UK: Oxford University Press.

Dondis, Donis A. 1973. *A Primer of Visual Literacy*. Cambridge, MA: MIT Press.

Doonan, Jane. 1993. *Looking at Pictures in Picture Books*. Stroud, UK: Thimble Press.

Eckert, Lisa Schade. 2006. *How Does It Mean? Engaging Reluctant Readers Through Literary Theory*. Portsmouth, NH: Heinemann.

Evans, Janet. 1998. *What's in the Picture? Responding to Illustrations in Picture Books*. London, UK: Paul Chapman.

Frye, Northrop. 1957. *The Anatomy of Criticism*. Princeton, NJ: Princeton University Press.

Genette, Gerard. 1999. *Palimpsets*. Translated by C. Newman and C. Doubinsky. Lincoln: University of Nebraska Press.

Gombrich, E. H. 1961. *Art and Illusion: A Study in the Psychology of Pictorial Representation*. 2d ed. Princeton, NJ: Princeton University Press.

Holland, Norman. 1975. *Five Readers Reading*. New Haven, CT: Yale University Press.

Iser, Wolfgang. 1978. *The Act of Reading*. Baltimore: Johns Hopkins University Press.

Jewitt, Carey, and Gunther Kress, eds. 2003. *Multimodal Literacy*. New York: Peter Lang.

Kiefer, Barbara Z. 1995. *The Potential of Picturebooks: From Visual Literacy to Aesthetic Understanding*. Englewood Cliffs, NJ: Prentice-Hall.

Kress, Gunther, and Theo van Leeuwen. 1996. *Reading Images: The Grammar of Visual Design*. London, UK: Routledge Falmer.

Labov, William, and Joshua Waletzky. 1967. "Narrative Analysis: Oral Versions of Personal Experience." In *Essays on Verbal and Visual Arts*, edited by J. Helm. Seattle: University of Washington Press.

Lewis, David. 2001. *Reading Contemporary Picturebooks: Picturing Text.* London, UK: Routledge Falmer.

Luke, Allan, and Peter Freebody. 1997. "Shaping the Social Practices of Reading." In *Constructing Critical Literacies: Teaching and Learning Textual Practice*, edited by S. Muspratt, A. Luke, and P. Freebody, 185–225. Cresskill, NJ: Hampton Press.

Myhill, Debra, Susan Jones, and Rosemary Hopper. 2006. *Talking, Listening, Learning: Effective Talk in the Primary Classroom.* Berkshire, UK: Open University Press.

Nikolajeva, Maria, and Carole Scott. 2006. *How Picturebooks Work.* New York: Routledge.

Nodelman, Perry. 1988. *Words About Pictures: The Narrative Art of Children's Picture Books.* Athens: University of Georgia Press.

Noell Moore, John. 1997. *Interpreting Young Adult Literature: Literary Theory in the Secondary Classroom.* Portsmouth, NH: Boynton/Cook.

Nystrand, Martin. 1997. *Opening Dialogue: Understanding the Dynamics of Language and Learning in the English Classroom.* New York: Teachers College Press.

Pearson, P. David, and M. C. Gallagher. 1983. "The Instruction of Reading Comprehension." *Contemporary Educational Psychology* 8: 317–44.

Peterson, Ralph, and Maryann Eeds. 1990. *Grand Conversations: Literature Groups in Action.* New York: Scholastic.

Serafini, Frank. 2001. *The Reading Workshop: Creating Space for Readers.* Portsmouth, NH: Heinemann.

———. 2004. *Lessons in Comprehension: Explicit Instruction in the Reading Workshop.* Portsmouth, NH: Heinemann.

Serafini, Frank, and Suzette Serafini-Youngs. 2006. *Around the Reading Workshop in 180 Days.* Portsmouth, NH: Heinemann.

Stewig, John Warren. 1995. *Looking at Picture Books.* Fort Atkinson, WI: Highsmith Press.

Tompkins, Jane, ed. 1980. *Reader-Response Criticism: From Formalism to Post-Structuralism.* Baltimore: Johns Hopkins University Press.

Vygotsky, Lev S. 1978. *Mind in Society: The Development of Higher Psychological Processes.* Cambridge, MA: Harvard University Press.

Wood, Diane, J. Bruner, and G. Ross. 1976. "The Role of Tutoring in Problem Solving." *Journal of Child Psychology and Psychiatry* 17: 89–100.

Children's Literature References

Ahlberg, Janet, and Allan Ahlberg. 1986. *The Jolly Postman or Other People's Letters*. Boston: Little, Brown.

Babbitt, Natalie. 1975. *Tuck Everlasting*. New York: Farrar, Straus & Giroux.

———. 1994. *Bub, or the Very Best Thing*. New York: HarperCollins.

Bang, Molly. 1999. *When Sophie Gets Angry—Really, Really Angry . . .* New York: Scholastic.

Base, Graeme. 1996. *The Discovery of Dragons*. New York: Viking.

Boyne, John. 2007. *The Boy in the Striped Pajamas*. New York: David Fickling Books.

Browne, Anthony. 1986. *Piggybook*. New York: Alfred A. Knopf.

———. 1990. *Changes*. New York: Farrar, Straus & Giroux.

———. 1997. *The Tunnel*. London: Walker Books.

———. 2001. *Voices in the Park*. New York: DK Publishing.

———. 2003. *The Shape Game*. New York: Farrar, Straus & Giroux.

———. 2004. *Into the Forest*. Cambridge, MA: Candlewick.

Bunting, Eve. 1994. *Smoky Night*. Illustrated by David Diaz. San Diego: Harcourt Brace.

———. 1998. *So Far from the Sea*. Illustrated by Chris Soentpiet. New York: Houghton Mifflin.

Burningham, John. 1977. *Come Away from the Water, Shirley*. London: Crowell.

———. 1978. *Time to Get Out of the Bath, Shirley*. London: Jonathan Cape.

Curtis, Christopher Paul. 1999. *Bud, Not Buddy*. New York: Random House.

———. 2004. *Bucking the Sarge*. New York: Random House.

DiCamillo, Kate. 2000. *Because of Winn-Dixie*. Cambridge, MA: Candlewick.

———. 2001. *The Tiger Rising*. Cambridge, MA: Candlewick.

———. 2003. *The Tale of Despereaux*. Cambridge, MA: Candlewick.

———. 2006. *The Miraculous Journey of Edward Tulane*. Cambridge, MA: Candlewick.

Fleischman, Sid. 1987. *The Whipping Boy*. Illustrated by Peter Sis. New York: Greenwillow Books.

Fox, Mem. 1997. *The Straight Line Wonder*. New York: Mondo.

Frank, Anne. 1991. *Diary of a Young Girl*. New York: Random House.

Gerstein, Mordicai. 2003. *The Man Who Walked Between the Towers*. Brookfield, CT: Roaring Brook Press.

Gravett, Emily. 2006. *Wolves*. New York: Simon & Schuster.

Hautman, Pete. 2004. *Godless*. New York: Simon Pulse.

Henkes, Kevin. 1991. *Chrysanthemum*. New York: Greenwillow Books.

———. 1993. *Owen*. New York: Greenwillow Books.

———. 1996. *Lilly's Purple Plastic Purse*. New York: Greenwillow Books.

Hesse, Karen. 1997. *Out of the Dust*. New York: Scholastic.

Hodges, Margaret. 1984. *Saint George and the Dragon*. Illustrated by Trina Schart Hymen. Boston: Little, Brown.

Howe, James. 1999. *Horace and Morris But Mostly Dolores*. New York: Atheneum Books for Young Readers.

Hutchins, Pat. 1968. *Rosie's Walk*. New York: Aladdin.

Innocenti, Roberto. 1985. *Rose Blanche*. New York: Creative Paperbacks.

Juster, Norton. 2005. *The Hello, Goodbye Window*. Illustrated by Chris Raschka. New York: Hyperion.

Kellogg, Steven. 1997. *The Three Little Pigs*. New York: William Morrow.

Kitamura, Satoshi. 1998. *Lily Takes a Walk*. New York: Sunburst.

Lester, Helen. 1988. *Tacky the Penguin*. New York: Houghton Mifflin.

———. 1995. *Listen Buddy*. New York: Scholastic.

———. 1999. *Hooway for Wodney Wat*. Boston: Houghton Mifflin.

Lorbiecki, Marybeth. 1998. *Sister Anne's Hands*. New York: Dial Books.

Martin, Janet Briggs. 1998. *Snowflake Bentley*. Boston: Houghton Mifflin.

McCully, Emily Arnold. 1992. *Mirette on the High Wire*. New York: Scholastic.

Mochizuki, Ken. 1993. *Baseball Saved Us*. New York: Lee & Low.

Polacco, Patricia. 2000. *The Butterfly*. New York: Philomel Books.

Portman, Frank. 2006. *King Dork*. New York: Delacorte Press.

Rappaport, Doreen. 2001. *Martin's Big Words: The Life of Dr. Martin Luther King Jr.* Illustrated by Bryan Collier. New York: Hyperion.

Rathmann, Peggy. 1995. *Officer Buckle and Gloria*. New York: G. P. Putnam's Sons.

Ringgold, Faith. 1991. *Tar Beach*. New York: Crown.

Ryan, Pam Muñoz. 1999. *Amelia and Eleanor Go for a Ride*. New York: Scholastic.

———. 2002. *When Marian Sang*. New York: Scholastic.

Rylant, Cynthia. 1998. *The Islander*. New York: DK Publishing.

Say, Allen. 1993. *Grandfather's Journey*. Boston: Houghton Mifflin.

———. 2002. *Home of the Brave*. New York: Houghton Mifflin.

Scieszka, Jon. 1994. *The Book That Jack Wrote*. Illustrated by Lane Smith. New York: Viking.

Sendak, Maurice. 1963. *Where the Wild Things Are*. New York: Harper & Row.

———. 1970. *In the Night Kitchen*. New York Harper & Row.

———. 1981. *Outside, Over There*. New York: HarperCollins.

Siebert, Diane. 2003. *Rhyolite: The True Story of a Ghost Town*. New York: Clarion.

Taback, Simms. 1999. *Joseph Had a Little Overcoat*. New York: Viking.

Thompson, Colin. 1988. *The Paradise Garden*. New York: Alfred A. Knopf.

———. 1993. *Looking for Atlantis*. New York: Random House.

Uchida, Yukio. 1993. *The Bracelet*. Illustrated by Joanna Yardley. New York: Philomel.

Van Allsburg, Chris. 1981. *Jumanji*. Boston: Houghton Mifflin.

———. 2002. *Zathura: A Space Adventure*. New York: Houghton Mifflin.

———. 2006. *Probuditi!* New York: Houghton Mifflin.

White, E. B. 1952. *Charlotte's Web*. New York: HarperCollins.

Wiesner, David. 2001. *The Three Pigs*. New York: Clarion Books.

Wild, Margaret. 1991. *Let the Celebrations Begin!* New York: Orchard Books.

Winter, Jeanette. 2005. *The Librarian of Basra*. Orlando, FL: Harcourt.

Woodson, Jacqueline. 2003. *Locomotion*. New York: Putnam.

Zelinsky, Paul O. 1997. *Rapunzel*. New York: Dutton.

Zolotow, Charlotte. 1962. *Mr. Rabbit and the Lovely Present*. New York: HarperCollins.

Zusak, Marcus. 2006. *The Book Thief*. New York: Arnold A. Knopf.

Around the Reading Workshop in 180 Days

A Month-by-Month Guide to Effective Instruction

Frank Serafini and **Suzette Youngs**

Picking up where *The Reading Workshop* and *Lessons in Comprehension* left off, *Around the Reading Workshop in 180 Days* gives you month-by-month strategies for running a reading workshop. Go *Around the Reading Workshop in 180 Days* with Frank and Suzette and take your students on a memorable journey into literacy.

2006 / 240pp / $27.00

978-0-325-00830-1 / 0-325-00830-2

Writing Without Boundaries

What's Possible When Students Combine Genres

Suzette Youngs and **Diane Barone**

With emphasis on choice, voice, and audience, *Writing Without Boundaries* familiarizes students with genres. It helps them understand how readers and writers use genre and how they can write on a topic from many perspectives. Read *Writing Without Boundaries* and show students how genres open a new world of possibilities for their writing.

2007 / 144pp / $18.50

978-0-325-01041-0 / 0-325-01041-2

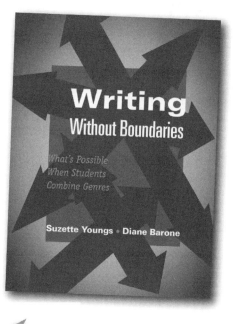

Sample Chapters
available online at
www.heinemann.com

To place an order, call 800.225.5800, or **fax 877.231.6980.**

www.heinemann.com